Praise for M

If examples, one-liners, stories, parables, illustrations, humor, and plain common sense are of interest and value to you, you will love MINDROBICS: HOW TO BE HAPPY FOR THE REST OF YOUR LIFE. Here is a book that really does have something for everybody. Young and old will benefit from this one. Steve Simms has a gem! I encourage you to benefit from this valuable information.

Steve Simms is a creative, articulate speaker and writer who has encouraged and inspired our people, both at meetings within our company and in articles he has written for our TOP PERFORMANCE magazine. He's easy to work with and a pleasure to know.

— ZIG ZIGLAR, motivational speaker, author, Chairman, The Zig Ziglar Corporation

*   *   *

In this day of constant negative media barrage, it is a pleasure and relief to find someone who can give me a daily positive approach. Steve Simms' MINDROBICS is that tool. A must read!

— SHEILA MURRAY BETHEL, speaker, author of the best-selling *Making a Difference, 12 Qualities That Make You a Leader*

*   *   *

An exciting book filled with great ideas to get motivated and stay that way. Profound enough to surprise a CEO, yet simple enough to create excitement in people who would never think that a book could improve their lives.

— GERHARD GSCHWANDTNER, founder and publisher of *Personal Selling Power* magazine.

Steve Simms teaches us how to "mind" our own business. Thanks to MINDROBICS, each of us can win the inner game that will lead to success in our outer world.

–DENNIS KIMBRO, speaker, author of the best-selling *Think and Grow Rich . . . A Black Choice.*

* * *

We become what we think about and are a result of the information we receive. MINDROBICS is full of refreshing, life-changing information that can play an important part in becoming the person you want to be.

–RUDY RUETTIGER, the inspiration behind the movie *Rudy* and inspirational-motivational speaker.

* * *

This is a wonderful book full of interesting, exciting ideas to brighten your mind and personality, and keep you positive and upbeat throughout the day. Everyone should read it!

–BRIAN TRACY, author, speaker, and CEO of Brian Tracy International

How To Be Happy
For The Rest Of Your Life

STEVE SIMMS

ALE

Attitude-Lifter Enterprises
528 Dale Court, Franklin, TN 37067

ISBN: 0-9648210-0-1

Cover design by Jim York
Produced by JM Productions, Brentwood, TN 37204

Attitude-Lifter Enterprises
528 Dale Court
Franklin, TN 37067

PRINTED IN THE UNITED STATES OF AMERICA

CONTENTS

Introduction. 1

1. What About That Self-Help Stuff? 9

2. Seven Benefits of a Happy Attitude 15

3. The Twenty-One Day Principle 21

4. Being Positive in a Negative World 25

5. Ten Myths About Happiness 33

6. At the Keyboard of Your Mind. 43

7. Understanding Fear and Anxiety 49

8. Anticipation, Not Anxiety. 57

9. Happiness Principles That Make Sense 63

10. Harness Your Thoughts 69

11. Enjoy Yourself While You're At It. 75

12. Seven Ways to Like Yourself Better. 79

13. Happy People Reject Mental Blueprints 89

14. Eight Practical Steps to Problem-Solving. 105

15. Don't Play the Blame Game 109

16. Happy People Enumerate Their Non-Financial Assets. 121

17. A Closer Look At MINDROBICS 133

18. Consciously Choose Optimism vs. Pessimism 145

19. Happiness in the Work Place 153

20. Go For It! 159

21. It's Your Party ... and You'll Laugh If You Want To! 167

DEDICATION

To my wife, Ernie, the love of my life, for her love, her tremendous belief in me, and for our "fantastic" marriage;

And

To my daughter Amelia, for her constant inspiration;

And

To my mother and father, Dot and Charlie Simms, for a lifetime of support, love, and encouragement.

ACKNOWLEDGMENTS

Thank you to the hundreds of self-help authors who have made a real difference in my life over the years.

Thank you to Sheila Murray Bethel, Gerhard Gschwandtner, Dennis Kimbro, Rudy Ruettiger, Brian Tracy, and Zig Ziglar for their encouragement and endorsements.

Thank you to Joseph S. (Joe) Johnson for his friendship and encouragement, and for his invaluable help in editing and revising my orginal manuscript.

Thank you to Dot Simms for her special help in getting this project off the ground.

And most of all, thank you to God for the unbounded love and blessings He has given me.

By shaping and transforming thoughts we free ourselves from their control. We are usually lived by our thoughts. They come to us, we accept them and they control us. Working on them, instead, gives us a sense of mastery.
— Piero Ferrucci

Being free from self-destructive behavior is not a mythological concept; rather, it's a real possibility.
— Wayne Dyer

It would be impossible to estimate the number of jobs that have been lost, the number of promotions missed, the number of sales blown, or the number of marriages ruined by poor attitudes.
—Dennis Kimbro

INTRODUCTION

THE HUMAN MIND is a wonderful thing, but like the human body, if it is neglected (if it is not fed a wholesome diet and given basic care and exercise) it becomes weak and sick. This book is an exercise program for the mind — your mind .

"Mindrobics" can be defined as: "Techniques for taking control of your mind and rigorously directing it down prescribed positive paths on a regular basis; systematically running upbeat thoughts through your mind." The goal of Mindrobics is happiness. Our method for achieving happiness will involve long-term, attitude-lifting techniques, rather than short-term hype.

"Oh, oh, here we go again!" With scads of books about happiness flooding the stores, both new and remainders, maybe that sums up your comment ... but hang on!

Even if you already consider yourself reasonably happy, wouldn't you like to be happy for the rest of your life? This book honestly spreads before you practical Mindrobics techniques for achieving success, contentment, satisfaction, and peace of mind—the main emotional and spiritual ingredients that make for genuine happiness.

1

Face it. Do you really know anyone who is exceptionally happy? I am referring to human beings. It would amaze you how many people can't think of anyone they assume is exuberantly happy. Every now and then in my seminars I encounter a few who can sort of conjure up one or two people who seem happy.

Happiness Is Within Your Control

How about yourself? Do you consider yourself a happy person? Most people think happiness is totally beyond their control and that it merely drops into their laps if they're fortunate enough. They feel happiness is what happens to them. Unfortunately for them, that is not the quotient for happiness.

Maybe none of us is able to discard all our preconceived notions, but at least in this book, let's try. Is it fair to ask that of you? I hope you're happy, full of confidence, and reasonably pleased with the direction of your life ... but all of us could stand to be happier, more confident, and more pleased with our lives. Some may feel happiness can never be theirs, and that it will always be out there somewhere beyond their grasp. If that is your situation, right this moment begin to cut that out of your thinking, because happiness can be yours—yes, yours.

Many of us simply choose to believe that our own life stories are produced by circumstances, directed by "fate," written by our families, and edited by our bosses. All too many of us have allowed ourselves to become victims. Instead of being stars in the galaxy, we think of ourselves as "poor me." When you think that long enough and strong enough, that's exactly what you'll be.

Share a Goal—Be Happier About Ourselves

I spell it out. My goal in Mindrobics is to learn to be happier about myself, my family, my vocation—happier about every facet of my life. In turn, I hope that as you read, you will join me in setting that as your personal goal.

Perhaps you're muttering, But, good grief, I've heard that before. Maybe you have in one form or fashion, but what have you done about it? You see, life is not something that merely happens to you. Life is something that you do. Life is given to us not just to be endured, but to be lived and to be enjoyed. You and I as human beings are unique among all the creatures on earth in that we can, except in the most extreme cases, help direct our lives and decide our fate.

Our thoughts and actions are not predetermined by blind instinct. They are our free choices to make. You and I can choose to be different or remain the same; choose to grow and develop or to stagnate; choose new paths or continually trudge on the familiar, but uninspiring, ground of tradition and habit.

Like the old folk song, "I'm just a piece of driftwood, and I'm drifting on," we can opt for existences (not really lives) devoid of direction, plans, and goals. One observer of life commented, "Everybody seems to be in such a hurry to get nowhere." Do you have the foggiest notion where you are going? Why not decide to aim for high ideals and point your life, like a guided missile, toward specific targets.

No doubt many thinkers have expressed this truism, "We have no choice but to choose." Right, you had nothing to do with coming into this world, but now that you are here, what you do with your life is a choice. You can choose to direct it or let it drift aimlessly. Don't expect another person to decide for you. Decide on the basis of your own heart and mind — not Mom or Dad or Dr. So-and-So or a counselor, a preacher or priest, a psychic, or a guru. You.

The Amazing Power to Choose

The power to choose may well produce fulfilling achievement, personal happiness, and an exhilarating life, whether you decide to fry chickens in a restaurant or fly different kinds of "birds" 35,000 feet up.

The failure to choose can mean barrenness, wretchedness, frustration, and anxiety, often asking yourself, "Why? Why?" And the ghosts of what might have been may end up tormenting you for the rest of your days. As John Greenleaf Whittier wrote, "The saddest words of tongue or pen are these: it might have been."

Beliefs, attitudes, and thoughts are not set in steel-reinforced concrete as many may presume. Your attitudes, thoughts, and feelings are immersed in the soft, tender gray matter of your brain. They can be removed, replaced, or adjusted with the freedom of choice. No, changing your mind-set is not easy — but a determined person, at any time, can decide to change or rearrange his life.

For instance, if you want to rearrange the furniture in your home, you can do it, even if you have to pay for assistance. You have the freedom to move the couch, chairs, lamps, rugs, and all the furnishings. But it will never happen if you sit down, twiddle your thumbs, and expect that furniture to rearrange itself! You have to follow up on the desire with a decision.

Changing your mind-set is not one bit different. It involves three plain elements: (1) Choice — making the decision to change; (2) Action — moving to implement the change; (3) Persistence — continuing to follow through on the desired action(s) until the sought-after change occurs. It is a tragedy that far too often people choose not to exercise their volition or will. Jane Taylor observed, "Though man, a thinking being is defined, few use the grand prerogative of the mind. How many never think who think they do."

Ride on Your Problems

More than likely friends and acquaintances have moaned to you, "I could be happy if I could only get rid of all my problems." You may have even thought that yourself. Are you living and breathing, even if you're not living and breathing too well? Then you're going to have problems.

Years ago there was a TV program in which a guy named Al would call his bookie, and his opening line always was, "Hello, Joe, This is Al. Got a problem!" That's one foible binding together the entire human race—problems. Problems are all around us. Sometimes in my speeches I ask the crowd, "Is there anyone here who has not had a problem in the past five years?" Pause. Nervous chuckle in the audience. Once in a while someone will raise their hand, and those sitting near that person will begin to snicker, and soon the entire crowd is laughing — because a fellow human being is claiming not to have experienced a problem within the last five years.

Problems (remember that problems may end up creating good for you rather than bad) are part and parcel of the human condition. All of us wish our problems would disappear, but they are tenacious as pit bulls.

Norman Vincent Peale was counseling a man who was complaining about his problems. Dr. Peale suggested, "Sir, I can take you to a group of people who have no problems." The man ecstatically replied, "That sounds wonderful. I'd like to see that group of people." Dr. Peale drove the man to a cemetery and remarked, "Now you can't see them, but just a little bit underground there's a whole group of people with no problems!" Peale made his point.

I personally believe that everybody either has a problem, is a problem, or is married to a problem! Try hard as we may, we cannot escape these blamed problems. Another anonymous philosopher said, "You're either in a problem, just leaving a problem, or headed toward a problem."

Don't Let Your Problems Drag You Down

That's often true of me. When I seem to dispose of one problem, there's another one looming on the horizon, and I never get rid of all my problems at one time. One rears its little head to replace the other...yet problems don't have to defeat us. One optimist said, "Every problem is an opportunity." And that's a fact. Another unknown sage expressed it, "Problems are inevitable, but misery is optional."

Don't let your problems drag you down. This is not a detailed introduction on problem-solving, but try not to panic over your problems. Most of them, believe it or not, are not as bad as we may think. Maybe a few of them are worse than we think. Yet, you and I can learn ways and means that will empower us rather than defeat us. Sadly, most unhappy people are looking at their problems from a totally negative slant, and that pulls them down. When people panic over their problems, they are often frozen with fear and inaction. They become emotionally and psychologically petrified, so they become powerless in confronting their problem(s).

One key is to prepare yourself for problems. Do not create them but anticipate how to react to them. Often problems arise, not to obstruct us, but to instruct us. If you honestly want happiness, you must stare this reality square in the face: a certain amount of problems are here to stay. If you and I are going to be happy, we can't do it in merely overcoming problems—but we can be happy in spite of them.

Learning from an Old Farmer

There's an old story about a farmer who certainly understood how to deal with problems. He was envied by his neighbors because he had one of the few horses in his village. Then one night his horse

5

jumped the fence and ran away. When the farmer's misfortune circulated the grapevine, his neighbors could hardly wait for the farmer's reaction.

They rushed to the envied farmer's door. When he greeted them, they shed crocodile tears with, "Oh, tssk, tssk, isn't this terrible!" With hardly the bat of an eyelash, the farmer replied stoically with one word,"Perhaps." The very next day the farmer's horse returned with three wild horses!

"How wonderful," his neighbors exulted. Again the farmer answered with that one word, "Perhaps."

The following day the farmer's son fell off one of the wild horses and broke his leg. So, his "comforters" showed up again and lamented, "Oh, how horrible! What a bad thing!" You guessed it—the old man answered, "Perhaps." The next day a military recruiter showed up at the village to draft all the young men for a war from which none of them returned alive, but the farmer's son was not drafted. He was spared because of his broken leg!

The moral? You are often not aware that in your life what seems bad today may turn out good tomorrow. Many seemingly dreadful, negative experiences are perhaps blessings in disguise. Now, I am sure, if you think back, you have seen that happen in your own life and career. Impossible situations, laden with doom and gloom, turned into serendipitous good fortune. You had thought, "Well, This is the last straw. I'm in the pits, and there's nothing I can do to change my cruel fate." But the situation did change for the better, and you might even have begun to believe in modern-day miracles.

I like Mark Twain's observation, "I'm an old man, and I've known many, many troubles, and yet most of them never happened." We amplify our troubles by expecting them and by worrying about them instead of facing up to the fact that troubles sometimes occur. They go with the territory. Troubles are a sign of life rather than a threat to life. If there were no problems or troubles, we would have no electricity, no automobiles, no airplanes, no computers, no radios, no televisions, no telephones, no modern conveniences. Every clever invention in the history of mankind was the product of a problem or trouble. So, why not cope with our problems and troubles as they arise and not submerge ourselves in moaning and groaning over them?

The Necessity of Problems ... or Learning from an Egg Shell

No doubt you have heard the story of the child who found a bird's nest. The child watched the baby bird trying to peck out of its shell. If you have ever watched this process, it is nature's picture of straining and struggling. It looks as though the "birdlet" will never emerge.

The child felt compassion for the bird, so he reached down with his hands and began to break the shell away piece by piece. Eventually, with both the bird and the child working, the bird exited his shell.

Those familiar with wildlife, though, realize that it is often better to "let nature take its course." The story has a sad ending because the bird soon died. Why? Because it was necessary for the bird to struggle so it could overcome the problem of the shell. In so doing the wee creature would have become better prepared to face the harshness of life outside of its shell. Because the child helped remove the obstacle the bird didn't have the strength to survive.

Hey, many of us refuse to cash in on our so-called problems, failing to realize—and I repeat—that "Every problem represents an opportunity." How could we possibly recognize a success if we never had a failure? How could we relish a win if we never lost? How could we feel good if we never felt bad? Huh? Munch on those questions. This is bizarre but nonetheless true. We need our problems so we can learn to deal effectively with life.

It seems every motivational-inspirational speaker must have a few poems at his disposal. Here's one that illustrates how problems mesh with happiness.

> It's easy to grin when your ship comes in
> And you've got the stock market beat.
> But the man worthwhile
> Is the lad who can smile
> When his shorts are too tight in the seat!

Doesn't that send ... chills up and down your spine?

My wife Ernie chided me for quoting that to an audience. "Steve," she cautioned, "I don't think you should use that poem, since the women will think it's sexist because it refers to a man with his shorts too tight!" So simply to be fair, I'll start talking about panty hose that fit too tight. What's my point? It's also uncomfortable to be happy and positive when so much around us is unhappy and negative.

So, what are we going to do amid all these problems? Will you follow me into Chapter 1, "What About That Self-help Stuff?"

You have the ability to change your world. Don't be afraid to start small, then go for greatness.

—Sheila Murray Bethel

Ideas are like wheelbarrows. They don't work unless you do.

—Anonymous

I am only an average man, but by George, I work harder at it than the average man.

—Teddy Roosevelt

1
WHAT ABOUT
THAT SELF-HELP STUFF?

RIGHT OFF THE BAT let's examine an extremely important Mindrobics principle. Are you ready for the shock?

Self-help material doesn't work!

Hold your horses, pilgrim! I can already hear you disgustedly asking yourself, "Why am I even holding this book in my hands if it doesn't work?" Undoubtedly you have heard that complaint before now: "That positive-thinking, self-help stuff just doesn't get the job done." Of course, I used to argue with those who made that statement ... but lately I've approached the subject from a different slant.

A real-estate broker once echoed those sentiments to me: "Look, Steve, that self-improvement crap just doesn't work." Those weren't idle words, he assured me, unlocking a filing cabinet and displaying only a part of motivational tapes for which he had paid 5,000 bucks!

Supposedly he had a treasure trove of inspiration and motivation under lock and key. Yet, by his own admission, he had gained practically nothing from the materials. Sad to confess, he doesn't lack for company. I'm sure you are acquainted with people who have bought tapes and books and have not profited from them.

As a speaker I've heard hundreds of reasons why self-help materials won't work. Many of the so-called reasons are mere excuses, but others may have validity. I have concluded that buying and collecting—and then reading, listening to, and viewing—self-help, self-improvement materials just doesn't do it! I hope I haven't burst your bubble.

Even this book, as good as I hope it is, won't make you happy by itself. Why won't self-help materials work? I repeat: why? Because they may just sit on a shelf or in a cabinet, collecting dust, powerless and helpless—that is, until a human being uses them, reads them, listens to them, and views them, sincerely applying the principles to his life.

The Crucial Key—Practice the Principles

Like a blueprint, a piece of self-help material is nothing but a suggested guide or map. In itself it is neutral. Unread, a book accomplishes zilch. One might as well use it as a door stop or a prop for a table leg. Neither can a blueprint ever erect a building. Human beings read books and complete edifices with hard work.

Now this may sound like double talk. Actually it's straight from the hip. Self-help guides will never produce self-help. All self-help is self-generated by self-effort—what we used to call "plain, old hard work."

People who think they can improve their lives merely by going through the mechanics—reading a book, listening to a tape, attending a seminar—are mistaken. Far too many look on self-help materials almost as good-luck charms, talismans, or even crystals, as if any of those actually make a difference.

The key to getting your money's worth out of self-help materials is: Self-help books, tapes, and seminars are only worth what you make them worth through your decision to apply yourself. "Achievement," the old adage goes, "is 1 percent inspiration and 99 percent perspiration." In other words, there's no Fairy Godmother. Yes, you can be happy. You can make yourself happier, and yet it won't happen with the snap of a finger and an incantation, "Zippo, Presto, Domino." I hate to disillusion you, but it will require hard work. When it comes to genuine, long-lasting self-improvement, nothing can substitute for dedication and effort.

Reads Easy—Does Hard?

Many critics of motivational materials have commented, "That stuff reads easy but does hard." That's nothing new, because self-improvement has always called for striving and struggling. There is a uniformity to truth, regardless of where it comes from. Epictetus wrote: "It's no easy thing for a principle to become a man's own unless each day he maintains it and works it out in his life."

Few people believe that personal perfection is attainable in this life. It is far down the pike for us, even though there is nothing wrong with wishing for it and aiming for it. Perfect happiness is also an unachievable goal in this "real world."

If we dwell on these stark realities and allow our lack of personal perfection and perfect happiness to discourage us, it can make us feel we have two-and-a-half strikes against us even before we step into the batter's box. On a ship in the Navy, when there is an urgent message, "Now hear this. Now hear this" comes over the speaker system. Readers, now hear this.

There is a positive side to our often negative human condition. So what if we're not perfect and we'll never be in this life! So what if a parent or a teacher or a person you thought was a friend insisted that you "toe the mark" toward perfection! Don't sweat it. One survey after another has proven that the most successful leaders in America are those who are willing to allow themselves and their followers or employees to fail now and then without suffering severe flagellation or firing. At one period or another, every successful person has failed. Edison, Lincoln, Einstein, Eisenhower, Katharine Hepburn. The list is legion.

You Can Be Happier Every Day

Now I want to make a note of this. If you are one of those who hate to mark up a book, OK—then write it on a pad or on the palm or your hand! You and I can do better every day. We can conscientiously embark on a program of personal improvement that will actually make us feel good about ourselves and others. We may not be able to be perfectly happy every day, of course, but we can be a little bit happier every day.

All of us know people who are absolutely crushed because they're not perfectly happy. For them it's "all or nothing at all." There is a touch of selfishness and self-pity in that attitude. They often convey the emotions of a kid on the playground, "If I can't be the quarterback, I'm gonna take my football and go home!" or, "If I can't be the mother, none of you can play with my doll!"

Another problem they have imposed on themselves is: they're aiming toward the wrong goal. They're trying to achieve perfect happiness instead of everyday happiness and a sense of satisfaction that comes mixed in with problems.

Even if we perceive of personal improvement as a minute, day-by-day effort, it's still difficult. I wouldn't dare deceive you into thinking it's a "snap." Many a person is creative but never ever steps out because they are afraid to dare. They are crawling with the sand crabs instead of soaring with the eagles because they are smart enough to realize that there is pain, sweat, and strain if one is to make accomplishments. So, they follow the line of least resistance. Nail it down—to improve yourself will call for drastically hard work, sometimes isolation, and even misunderstanding from family and friends, if you have them. To become happier and to improve requires—ugh—work.

So Why Try?

So why bother since self-help is so difficult? Why try? Quite frankly, most people don't. That is also why polls have revealed that 65 percent of all workers are dissatisfied with their jobs. I have known mechanics who wanted to be sculptors, fry cooks who wanted their own restaurant, and many more with a seemingly "Impossible Dream" ... but they were scared to break loose and go for it.

Somehow I am convinced you want to advance, or you probably wouldn't be reading this book. But let me make an analogy. Suppose a benefactor offered you $10 million, tax-free and in cash, if you would consistently be happy for thirty days, would you give it a try?

You might reply, "But how would that person know if I'm happy or not?" Here's the catch. They're going to interview your husband or wife, your kids, your friends, your boss, your co-workers, people who relate to you socially, and those who come in contact with you at religious organizations or civic clubs. They're going to follow behind you at the end of thirty days and interview everybody in your life. If a single soul reports, "No, he's not happy," you would forfeit the $10 million. If everybody says, "Yes, he's been the happiest he's ever been during the last thirty days," you would keep the windfall.

Would you take them up on that? You know what. I can imagine for that kind of money you could convince the folks around you that you were happy—and yet I doubt if you will ever have an offer like that.

Happiness and Love Are Not for Sale

Literature is full of stories about the fact that riches cannot buy happiness. Think about mythical King Midas who was granted his wish that all he touched would turn to gold. His life became wretched as he hugged his daughter, and she was transformed into a gold ingot. He broke his teeth on golden food; his capital city was "solid gold." Finally, in sheer desperation, he even begged for poverty. His second wish was also granted, and he became happy with the smallest things—the hug of a warm, flesh-and-blood daughter, cold beans on a pewter platter, and even weeds in his yard.

So many people in Western culture have equated happiness with wealth. Many of the wealthiest people in history have been poverty-stricken emotionally. The late J. Paul Getty in the early 1960s was considered the richest man in America, perhaps in the world. In his memoirs he wrote, "I could wish that I had married happily. Instead I have gone through five marriages... . I am not a happy man." Howard Hughes's fate also speaks volumes about the naked reality that money cannot buy happiness. As someone said, "Money doesn't buy happiness. It just helps you to select the misery you enjoy!"

This is simplistic but true. There are fantastic benefits to being happy, benefits that outweigh all the precious metals and jewels in the world. Read on.

There is no beautifier of complexion, or form, or of behavior, like the wish to scatter joy and not pain around us.

—Virgil

Happiness is its own reward.

—Anonymous

To strive with difficulties and to conquer them is the highest human felicity.

— Samuel Johnson

2
SEVEN BENEFITS
OF A HAPPY ATTITUDE

W HY SEVEN BENEFITS? Why not 700? My chapter simply came together with seven benefits, not forty like Ali Baba and his thieves.

1. *The first benefit of being happy is the sheer thrill of it.* It's exciting to feel good. Happiness is its own reward. Frankly, I try not to let my limitations impede me from moving forward and planning ahead. At times my own shortcomings are my worst bugaboos, but I cannot afford—neither can you—to let the gremlins of doubt and insecurity block my performance.

You and I must passionately believe that—if anyone else has ever overcome his inner weaknesses, fears, anxieties, and troubles, and learned to live a happy life, then we can, too. This positive attitude challenges me to keep hurdling the obstacles that would thwart my quest for self-improvement. There's nothing like the ecstatic thrill of overcoming a personal hang-up.

Samuel Smiles, wrote a book back in 1859, called *Self Help*. He noted: "The spirit of self-help is the root of all genuine growth in the individual. Help from without is often enfeebling in its effects, but help from within invariably invigorates." I have discovered that, when I help myself to grow, to improve, to be happier, to be more positive, I experience such a thrill—there's nothing like it.

Unless my wife, Ernie, notices when I beat back a negative mind-set that has attacked my mind for a day or longer, no one else does. Yet, when that happens, I want to celebrate like the winners of the Super Bowl and the World Series. Talk about invigoration and being "turned on," there is a supercharged high from working to be happy.

2. *Your self-improvement and happiness not only help you but also those around you.* One anonymous student of life has pointed out that "there's only one corner of the world you can be sure of improving, and that's your own self." Think of the difference it would make if more and more people would strive for self-improvement. There's an old song that goes, "Give to the world the best you have, and the best will come back to you." That is an irrefutable truth.

Now I am not going to wait for others to become dedicated to happiness and self-improvement. If I do I might have to wait a long, long time. But if I start to improve myself, then when I get better, my family's better, my wife's better, my associates are better. When you fix yourself and when you're happier, you affect those around you. Sometimes your best means of helping other people is first to help yourself. Then all of the positive influences of your life will have a tendency to rub off on even your casual acquaintances. Don't you love being around positive people? Wouldn't you rather be in the company of "Happy" than "Grumpy"? Perhaps the best gift you can give your family and friends is a positive and happy you!

3. *Self-confidence is another benefit.* A positive attitude builds self-confidence like nothing else. As you become happier, your confidence level will rise.

Remember that even the person who seems to exude self-confidence has his carefully covered moments of insecurity and instability. In fact, the guy who oftentimes spouts off about his all-conquering confidence is actually a sheep in wolf's clothing. Instead of howling, deep down inside he is going "baaa." False bravado accomplishes nothing.

Instead, "keep on keeping on." Make up your mind to do better and determine to be happy, come hell or high water, and you will begin to store up a reservoir of confidence. As you overcome one problem, you will become a bit more confident. Then as you succeed with another dilemma, you will become stronger. Now you will never make the mistake of thinking you are "invincible," to quote from an old Helen Reddy song, but you will become characterized by confidence and a sense of well-being. And you will begin to believe in yourself and think, "I have something to offer after all! I can not only make it, but I can make it effectively and successfully!"

4. *Fantastic human relations will result.* Without fail, those who are happy and positive seem to have better relationships than those who aren't. I have heard the remark, "If you're miserable, don't feel sorry for yourself. Feel sorry for the person who has to live with you!" That's the absolute truth.

Determine that you yourself are not going to be miserable and that you're not going to make others miserable either. You have heard that "misery loves company." The bare fact is, though, that most company doesn't love misery. Chronically miserable people don't have friends and would-be friends lining up at their doors.

If you'll "accentuate the positive, eliminate the negative, and latch on to the affirmative," you will fortify friendships. Those who want to enjoy life might well seek you out, maybe even for somewhat selfish reasons, because you make them feel good about themselves and about life. You were put here not only to have happiness for yourself but also to spread it onto your family, your friends, and all others with whom you come in contact.

5. *Improved performance will follow.* All available data seem to indicate that happy people are more fruitful and productive. I will not argue with the few exceptions to the rule.

By and large, when you are happy in your work, you tend to produce more. Even though perks, working conditions, and pay raises are pivotal, sometimes your highest happiness lies in being able to end the work day with the feeling of satisfaction, "Today I've given it my best." Managers, if your employees are happy they will function more efficiently and productively.

Experts report that a person's attitude is one of the three top ingredients involved in success and production. These three are talent, practice, and attitude. You ought to possess all three, of course, but best-selling author Charles Swindoll has written that attitude accounts for 85 percent of success or failure in life—85 percent! So, when your attitude is optimistic and upbeat, your whole level of production will be up, and you'll be on a roll.

6. *Other practical benefits are increased income and various material rewards.* This is not written from a "gimme, gimme" standpoint, but if you share happiness, friends will certainly find it easier to appreciate you and like you more. Face it. An old proverb goes, "Cast your bread on the waters, and it will come back to you one hundred-fold." Your friends, quite frankly, will want to do more for you, even though you may not even ask them.

Unless your boss is a veritable Attila the Hun, he will probably want to do more for you if he possibly can. Raises. Benefits. Perks. Commendations. Like it or not, we are dependent on other people. John Donne aptly wrote, "No man is an island unto himself."

Yes, not only emotional and psychological rewards will land in your lap, but also material rewards. It's plain as the nose on an elephant. Since most of what we receive comes from people, the more people like us, the more inclined they are to do for us. If you are in sales, customers will buy more from you. Regardless of your occupation, people will seek you out.

They will even recommend you. "Hey, you ought to contact Jane Doaks. She's a joy to work with. She's dependable, honest. Here's her card. I keep a few extra around. She can find the real estate you're looking for. My wife and I think she's the best, and we recommend her without hesitation."

"George Doaks is the best mechanic I've ever run into. He's not a whole lot cheaper than the others, but it's the way he treats you. You know, you've been to mechanics who think they're doing you a big favor to take your money and then grumble and grunt while they finish your work. Not George. He's not just interested in your car. He's interested in you, and he wants you to feel good about everything." People like Jane and George have more satisfaction, but also make more money because of their outlook on life.

7. *Another benefit is better health.* More and more research reveals that nothing can affect your overall health like attitude. In fact, a bad attitude breeds sickness. As an unknown genius has put it: "The surly bird gets the germ."

And if you're dejected, rejected, and neglected—and always feeling down and out—you will not only help make others sick, but you yourself will be sick. Sure, all of us will become sick sometimes, and, yes, we will die eventually. But there is nothing like being positive to give us longer life, better health, and less expenses, especially from psychosomatic illnesses.

A positive attitude and a spirit of joy are better pain relievers than all the analgesics and blockers on the market. An upbeat mental attitude strengthens the body's immune system and releases into the mind and nervous system a natural drug that's more powerful than morphine. It can give you a "natural high." It's wonderful to be happy. By now I hope you're at least a little bit convinced from these seven benefits to conclude, "Maybe you're onto something here! I'd like to pursue this."

Stop right this moment! This book cannot in itself guarantee you happiness. Remember, "this self-help stuff doesn't work." No, you have to work it. You might comment, "But, Steve, I've tried all of this—positive thoughts, good attitude, the pursuit of happiness—but things haven't worked out exactly as I had hoped."

I've had those feelings myself, but that doesn't mean for you and me to quit. If you follow the principles of Mindrobics, they might well amaze you.

We must make our habits, and then our habits make us.
—John Dryden

Every good that is worth possessing must be paid for in strokes of daily effort.

—William James

If you learn what you have to do to be successful and then do it consistently until it becomes a habit, you can achieve anything you want in life. There are no limitations on the outside, only on the inside.

—Brian Tracy

3
THE TWENTY-ONE DAY PRINCIPLE

OH, MAN, WHAT ARE we into now? Maybe that's your question only a few pages into the book, but this is urgent if you're planning on enjoying happiness, emotional stability, better health, and a genuine sense of well-being.

Twenty-one days. That may seem long at the moment, but that's only three calendar weeks—only 5.9 percent of an entire year. What do you have to lose?

Do You Really Mean Business?

Let's hope you are revved up and ready to put Mindrobics techniques into practice. Are you persistent? Do you want happiness and success? Now, you're going to try these principles. Candidly, I must write: they're not going to work the first time. Unless you stick with these, they aren't going to do you a bit of good.

There's another reason for that, and that's because it requires twenty-one days in which to change behavior.

Are you outrageously happy yet? You've gone this far in the book. Has it already worked? I hope you're not expecting a miracle that quickly because it's a verified fact psychologically that it takes three weeks, twenty-one days—don't ask me why—to change an attitude, a thought pattern or mind-set, or a behavior.

The reason most people give up on self-help is: they start on it and try five minutes, ten minutes, maybe a day or two. Then they throw up their hands and quit without giving the principles or program a chance. And they scream bloody murder, "It just doesn't work. It's simply another bunch of head games." That's neither fair to themselves nor to the concerned person who offers the self-improvement materials.

Driving—Not Miss Daisy—But Driving Whoever

Presuming that you probably drive a vehicle—a car, van, truck, bus, RV—can you recall when you were learning to drive? I still develop goose bumps when I remember picking up my learner's permit at 15, so my dad, in fear and trembling, set out to teach me. That fateful day arrived when I sat behind the wheel of that straight-shift car (I hope you were spared that trauma and learned on an automatic transmission).

I was nervous as I tried to put my parents' automobile into reverse. To put it mildly, it was like breaking a bucking bronco for the rodeo. Finally, I ground that machine into reverse, let up on the clutch, and that car lunged backwards, quivering and sputtering, finally gasping and dying. Dad was becoming rather red-faced and upset with me. And guess what? I naturally began to feel negative emotions. It was my first time, but dire negativisms were racing up and down my system, "This is the end of the world. I'll never be able to drive. No self-respecting girl will ever date me, because she'll be able to drive, and I won't. The kids at school will laugh at me." I was defeating myself even before I had honestly begun ... but doesn't that happen to all of us at every stage from childhood through old age?

Yes, I was embarrassed, discouraged, and humiliated, yet I kept struggling—and guess what. In ten minutes I finally drove out into the street, and it probably took me about thirty minutes to drive around the block. When I finally made it back home, I was so pooped I shouted, "I'm not cut out for this driving mess!" And I've never driven since.

Now if you believe that, I want to sell you a tract of choice oceanfront property in Iowa. In spite of the hassle, I kept on with it.

Yet, all too many people give up almost before they begin to try. They'll have one negative experience and "throw in the towel," moaning, "I'm not cut out for that. I'm doomed to be unhappy and unsuccessful. Poor me." Have you either thought or spoken those words? They're not true! If you have trouble implementing certain techniques, it doesn't mean you're not cut out for it. It merely signifies that you can't do it in one experience or in one day.

The following day, with grim determination I climbed into that car again, even though I dreaded it. I was a teenage mass of nerves, all thumbs and clumsy—but I persisted. I sort of felt like that car was a girl; I was timid around them too. I practiced driving one week and then two weeks. It wasn't easy. I especially had trouble climbing hills when trucks were stopped there, and my coordination was clunky. Seriously, though, I have never known of anything worthwhile that was always easy and free of trouble.

Fortunately I didn't quit. By the end of three weeks I had become a driver—twenty-one days. And I've been driving ever since. Now my driving is second nature. I drive without even thinking about it!

It Takes a While to Change

Compute it into your mind: It takes a while to change a behavior or a pattern. If you're often sad, depressed, and negative, remember that those are learned and cultivated behaviors. They can be changed with the Mindrobics techniques we're going to examine in this book. They can be changed but not overnight.

Give It Twenty-one Days

Are you game? For genuine happiness and a better life, are you willing to work at changing yourself for twenty-one days? That's all. I am asking only that you pick out two or three techniques from this book and really work on them for three calendar weeks.

At the end of twenty-one days, they will start to kick in, and you will sense that you are actually changing. Your friends and acquaintances will notice you are changing. As that happens in your life, your self-confidence will build up and accelerate. And if you follow these techniques, you will become addicted to a life that will make you glad you're alive. In fact, you may begin to approach each day with anticipation, "Well, I wonder what fantastic surprises are

23

in store for today? I can hardly wait!" You will have begun to "accentuate the positive" instead of the negative.

Everybody Needs Improvement

Years ago I started using self-help tapes and books and going to inspirational-motivational seminars. Why? Because I'm patently human and realized it, and I had undergone enough letdowns and put-downs to last for a lifetime. How would I improve my situation? By improving myself—that's how. Admittedly, reading, listening, and being a spectator were simple, but following through was hard work for a number of weeks. Then I became caught up not only in improving myself but also helping others to do likewise. Those materials—call them what you will—helped me to recognize it is far better to "light a candle than to curse the darkness."

Even though I am a full-time motivational-inspirational speaker, I am still a "fan" of other self-help, self-improvement speakers and writers like Zig Ziglar, Robert H. Schuller, and Norman Vincent Peale. Remember, too, that effective self-improvement will aid others all around you. If your self-help or improvement ends with you, it has not accomplished its most rewarding purpose. I make no bones about it. I am into that kind of material because I want a better me, a better you, and a better world around us.

So, now let's zero in on ...

Everybody in the world is seeking happiness—and there is one sure way to find it. That is by controlling your thoughts. Happiness doesn't depend on outward conditions. It depends on inward conditions.

—Dale Carnegie

Your mind is what makes everything else work.

—Kareem Abdul-Jabbar

To what is good I open the doors of my being and jealously shut them against what is bad.

—Helen Keller

4

BEING POSITIVE IN A NEGATIVE WORLD

or

The Saga of a Marble

ONE CRITIC OF POSITIVE THINKING facetiously commented, "I'm positive about one thing, this world is negative." He was correct only from the slant of a pessimist.

The Three E's of Encouragement

How can we be positive with so many negative influences and pessimistic people crawling out of the woodwork? Believe me, it's not a cinch. Right here I want to present a concept that has become a dynamic force in my life. I call it ... "The Three E's of Encouragement."

To make my point about The Three E's of Encouragement, it is essential that I relate a personal story. The reason I make mention of my experience is: most people think the way you feel is totally beyond your control. They excuse a violent temper or a bad mood with, "I

25

just can't help my feelings." Maybe you adhere to that. If you've lived long enough, I bet you've heard that a thousand times, often after you have suffered from another person's anger or mean attitude.

Engineering Your Feelings

I hope this story points out that you can engineer your feelings. It's unusual how most of us want to engineer and change our circumstances, yet practically none of us want to change ourselves and alter our emotions. As Shakespeare would express it, "Aye, there's the rub."

This story springs from my early days of professional speaking. I presented a speech to a marketing association and used one of my favorite principles concerning a positive attitude: You can feel however you want to feel, regardless of your circumstances or surroundings. That, to me, is the bedrock foundation of happiness—coming to the point where you are fully aware your happiness is up to you. "If it is to be, it's up to me."

You can engineer your thoughts and the inner workings of your mind to the extent you can feel however you want to feel. Hear me out. Have you put that into practice? Then, I ask you not to criticize it if you haven't utilized it.

That wintry night, in the Christmas season, I left the marketing seminar feeling great as I headed for my home on the side of a hill in Brentwood, Tennessee. On the 10 o'clock news the weatherman predicted snow and ice for the night. That rang a bell in my cranium. "Steve, when there's snow and ice you can't get your car out of the driveway. Remember?"

Of course, I, like you, strive to avoid negative situations. Right. I'm neither a masochist nor a martyr. I'm not into pain and problems, but you've already figured that out by now. I didn't want my car stuck in the driveway, and I didn't want to be stuck either, so I parked it on the road where I could still drive it on level ground.

The following morning I awoke to a winter wonderland. And to what did my wondering eyes appear? Not a jolly old elf and eight tiny reindeer. Instead I was greeted with inches of ice on the driveway. But I was so smart. If I hadn't parked the car on the road, I would have been stranded. Oh yes, when you win one, it feels good, doesn't it? Sometimes I love to beat circumstances.

I was perkier than my percolator. I dressed for success that day and began sort of skating on my driveway. As I reached the car door I noticed that the driver's side window had a hole in it about the size of an orange. All around that hole the glass was shattered. As I opened the door the entire window fell into the front seat. Now you may not believe it, but I actually began to feel negative emotions.

The first insane thought that popped into my head was: "Get a gun, lie under the car, and wait for the dude who did this." I never have even owned a gun. I hate violence, but I began to feel violent as my eyes bulged and the veins stood out on the side of my neck. To put it mildly, I was frustrated, mad, hurt, and almost totally steeped in negatives. It was a "Maalox moment."

Of course I realized that I had no right to be considering shooting a guy simply because he had broken my window. I eliminated that option rather quickly. Then a dirty little gremlin, in the form of a negative, traipsed across the backroads of my mind: "Well, you deserve a bad day today. Yesterday was a triumph, so today's the bottom of the dumpster. This is terrible. Rotten. Why did this happen to me? Poor me!" My stomach was so upset I thought of taking Tums, Kaopectate, and Pepto-Bismol.

Down on my hands and knees in the car, I searched for the problem. On the floorboard I found it—a small glass marble with a chip on it, not nearly as large as the chip on my shoulder! Evidently the culprit had done it with a slingshot or some sort of gun. I never liked to play marbles that much anyhow because I usually lost all my marbles—and again I was doing exactly that, losing all my marbles.

The danger of teaching positive thinking, as I do, is that you are often called on to eat your own words. As I fumed and made a mountain out of a marble, I remembered what I had said to the marketing association the day before. "You can feel however you want to feel, regardless of your circumstances."

"What a hypocrite!" I thought to myself, "Oh, no, yesterday you told your audience that you can engineer your attitude and that you can be happy, in spite of the circumstances."

Enter the Three E's of Encouragement

Rather than cringe at even the thought of adversity, why not join me in calling these storms **events-that-activate**? This is the first E in the Three E's of Encouragement. Why do I call them that? Because they often activate you in mind, body, and soul. Maybe it seems for a few days or longer, you are leading a charmed life—no fuss, no muss, no bother, no sweat, no strain. Then, splat, it hits the fan. It may seem for a while that nothing goes right, and you ask yourself all kinds of probing, even philosophical, questions. You feel like a biblical Job, Jr.

Perhaps a co-worker is giving you a hard time, maybe even trying to make you look bad so he may be promoted instead of you. Or you and your spouse argue about the children, money, your dwelling, your car, sex, *ad infinitum*. Or your boss chews you out, sometimes because his boss has done that to him, and his boss has done that.

Again, those events-that-activate are represented by the first E in the Three E's of Encouragement. The event in my story was the marble through my car window. A little glob of glass activated me. Of course, there was nothing I could have done to prepare for that stupid marble except bullet-proof glass. It was too late to do anything about it, except to have a new window installed.

Far too many of earth's citizens will spend years worrying over circumstances and events that are past, and all the anguish and pain are doing nothing but making life unbearable.

The second E in the Three E's of Encouragement is for the **evaluation**. The event was the marble through the window. The evaluation was what I was thinking about it. My evaluation at the time was: "This is terrible. Seek revenge on the dude who did it. It shouldn't have happened to me. Why couldn't it have happened to my neighbor instead of me?" At the moment I nursed a passel of illogical, irrational beliefs—over a marble. Yes, I'm ashamed to admit that I am capable of such exaggerated thoughts … but all of us are.

Then the third E came into play. It stands for **emotions,** my negative emotions, involving my overreaction to the situation. My entire chemistry was out of kilter. Your mind affects your body. Innumerable books and articles have been written on the subject of mind over matter and psychosomatic medicine. At one time it was estimated that about 80 percent of all hospital patients had nothing physically wrong with them. (S. I. McMillen's *None of These Diseases* is a classic on the subject. It is still in print.) When we harbor negative emotions, they may affect every function of our bodies. The most respected doctors in medicine report that a healthy, positive-thinking mind is the surest safeguard of overall bodily health. But if a person continues to pet and stroke dark, negative feelings, he will literally become physically sick. The third E is for the emotions.

What Makes Us Feel Bad?

The emotions in my case were unpleasant. Now hang in there with me. Most people think that negative emotions emanate from the events-that-activate in their lives. The broken window didn't actually make me feel bad. What made me emotionally upset was my evaluation of the situation.

As I held that marble I was thinking, "Hey, you shouldn't be feeling this way. You shouldn't be so upset, because you just told a group that one can feel however he wants to feel." Then I asked myself, "How can I fix this?" I call this approach "attitude engineering."

It was too late to deal with the activating event, so I switched to my evaluation that the marble event was dreadful. Then I inquired of myself, "Is there anything you can change to make yourself believe that there is something good about that marble busting your window?" I earnestly tried to change my negative evaluation.

What's Good About the Situation?

When you have an activating event in your life, here's an excellent Mindrobics technique to change your evaluation. Ask yourself, "What's good about it?" I'm not kidding. No matter what happens in your life, somewhere, somehow there's bound to be something good about it! Literary scholars concur that John Milton wrote his greatest poetry after his blindness. Musicologists agree that Ludwig von Beethoven composed his greatest symphonies after his deafness. Those and untold multitudes of others have asked themselves, "What's good about it?" They turned the seemingly bad into good and enriched the lives of millions. They found good even in pain, suffering, deprivation, and disabilities.

At this point you may think I have truly lost my marbles. No way. If you'll only search, you can discover the good. If you expect the bad, of course you will always find it.

So I repeated the question, "What's good about this lousy marble? How can I evaluate it positively?"

Since it was early in my career as a professional speaker I began to envision myself before groups of people—and even crowds. I would relate the story of my Maalox-moment marble and use it as the prop and as an object lesson for The Three E's of Encouragement.

The marble also created dreams, not of the impossible kind, either, and goals for my career. Many people are "groupies" or at least fans for rock stars, Hollywood celebs, and sports heroes. Me, I'm a fan of motivational speakers. I thought: "I don't know a speaker in the country who has a marble. They will all be jealous of me!"

The more I focused on the good things about that marble, the better I began to feel. I actually began to "bond" with that marble I had once felt was terrible. Would you believe I began to like it? My window was still demolished. Nothing had changed but the way I looked at the situation. And yet, my emotions changed from negative to positive because I had changed my evaluation!

Avoid the Lapses

Back inside the house I pulled out my insurance policy—probably shouldn't have done that because I found out there was a $100 deductible on my comprehensive. All of a sudden I blurted out, "Oh, no. This is terrible. A hundred bucks for a stinking marble!" Now you know exactly what happened, don't you? As I indulged myself in those thoughts, I began feeling rotten again.

I had lapsed into the event-that-activates programming where I keyed in on the negatives and let them zap me with bad feelings. This time the event was the statement in the insurance policy that my insurance would not cover the entire window and that I would have to cough at least $100.

Of course, I was repeating that doleful litany, "This is bad. This is terrible. This is gross. This is ..." — as a result of my evaluation or perception of my predicament. Thus the negative emotions refiltered through my system.

The event this second time was the lack of insurance coverage. The evaluation was: this is bad for me. The emotions were negative.

I deliberately put a stop to those patterns of thinking and gained control of my mind by talking with myself. "No, I'm not going to think like that. It's worth the $100." Right on the spot I changed my evaluation. I couldn't change the fact, but I changed the evaluation. When I altered that, the bad emotions disappeared.

I like my that marble and still use it as my "straight man" in my speeches. It's been an asset to my speaking career.

How to Use the Three E's of Encouragement

When you are activated by an event:

1. Ask yourself, "What is the event-that-is-activating me?"

2. Ask yourself, "What is my evaluation of this event? What am I telling myself?"

3. Ask yourself, "Are the emotions I am feeling helping me? Do I like them?"

If you answered no to the questions in 3., proceed to 4.

4. Ask yourself, "How can I change my evaluation into something positive? What is good about this event?" Then use your imagination. Be creative. Be determined! Find some good things about the event.

5. Choose to think about the positive evaluation! Reject the negative evaluation. Persist!

6. If you persist thinking about the positive evaluations and reject the negative evaluations, soon your emotions about the event will change from harmful to helpful!

You shall know the truth and the truth will set you free.
                                                                    –Jesus

*If any be unhappy, let him remember that he is unhappy
by reason of himself alone.*

                                                            —Epictetus

*We ought to be as cheerful as we can; if only because to
be happy ourselves is a most effective contribution to the
happiness of others.*

                                                    —Sir John Lubbock

5
TEN MYTHS ABOUT HAPPINESS

NEGATIVISM IS PART and parcel of flawed human existence.
In every civilization, bar none, there are negative persons in all areas
of life, in Bangor, Maine, and Bangladesh; in Waterproof, Louisiana,
and Warsaw, Poland; in Bull Frog Corner, Mississippi, and
Bucharest, Romania.

There is no subject causing more confusion than the meaning of
happiness. What is happiness? What is its origin? What does one do
in order to gain and possess happiness? Many question whether
anyone can be truly happy.

In our Western culture we are confronted with a variety of
unsound, twisted ideas of happiness and what it constitutes. Here I
examine ten myths, or false concepts, of happiness in our society.
Every one of them ought to be exposed for what they are, so people
can change and then have reasonably happy and productive lives.

Myth Number One: Never-Never Land

This is the mistaken notion that long-lasting happiness is not
possible here in the real world. At face value those who adhere to this
idea declare, "You're just not going to be happy over the long haul,
so don't expect to be. Life is merely a series of farces and tragedies,

33

but go for what little bit of happiness you can ... but all happiness is fleeting and tenuous. It's impossible to be happy here in this concrete, tangible world."

Fortunately, that is a myth. The Bible makes a statement about people being able to have "strong delusion that they would believe a lie." However, if you believe a myth, even a lie, long enough, it can seem to become a reality for you. If you hold to the myth that you can never be happy here, then no matter what activating event happens in your life, you are not going to have positive emotions.

Your false and negative belief will destroy whatever chance you have for happiness here in this life. This myth can snuff out one's desire to live and can strangle hope, for this is a myth that smacks of hopelessness. "You can't be happy so you can't even try for it. Accept your dismal fate as it is." Many cannot live with such kismet, so they send up with a death wish, whether or not it is ever carried out.

Myth Number 2: The Bluebird of Happiness

This myth contends that a person has little or no control over whether or not he or she is happy. Happiness whimsically comes and goes on its own. Folks all around us believe that poppycock.

They believe that happiness merely lights on your shoulder and that you have no say-so about it. Cross your fingers, carry a rabbit's foot, and hope to your lucky stars that happiness graces you, but you have absolutely no control over it. If you buy that, you have given up control, so you no longer try to engineer your happiness but, as with Myth 1, you yield to your "fate." You may or may not be happy, and you have nothing to do with it. What have you done? You have allowed yourself to become a victim.

Myth Number 3: Piggyback Happiness

This false concept pushes the idea that it is virtually impossible to be happy when everything is not going well in a person's life. To be happy, according to this view, a person must have a constant succession of happy happenings.

In other words, you cannot be happy unless "good stuff" is occurring in your life almost non-stop. Likewise, all of your activating events have to be positive, or you can't be happy. That's also a dead-end trap, and it just isn't so!

Myth Number 4: Catch the Carrot

This myth postulates that it is nearly impossible to achieve happiness. Thomas Jefferson, himself a carrot-topped revolutionary, penned these lines in the Declaration of Independence:

> We hold these truths to be self-evident: that all men are created equal, that they are endowed by their Creator with certain inalienable rights, that among these are life, liberty, and the pursuit of happiness... .

And how! "The pursuit of happiness." One of our founding fathers was indicating that happiness is actually hard to achieve—that we must pursue it pantingly and breathlessly. We must chase after it even as mules galloped after a dangled carrot in those races of yore or as greyhounds scurry after a mechanical rabbit at the dog track. The mules and greyhounds discovered that the carrot or rabbit were always one stride ahead of them, unreachable, uncatchable.

All around us are people trying to catch "the elusive butterfly" Bob Lind sang about in the 1960s. The idea that happiness is unattainable tramples the human spirit and causes people to lose hope. When hope is gone, one might as well give up. This theory, too, is a delusion. It is a myth producing dire consequences in one's heart and mind.

Myth 5: Happy Days

Quite frankly this is one of the silliest of the happiness myths. It operates on the premise that some days are happy, and some days are sad or bad. Days in themselves are neither happy nor unhappy. They have no emotions. We have the emotions. A day simply is. That's all there is to it. Let me repeat: there are no glad days. There are no sad days. There are glad and sad people. Regardless of what happens, it doesn't have to make you unhappy.

My tried-and-true contention is that you can be happy in spite of what happens to you. In fact, many of those with the worst adversities were happiest not in spite of, but because of their adverse circumstances. I could fill this entire book with cases of blind, deaf, mute, crippled, and otherwise disadvantaged persons who drank the cup of happiness to the fullest.

Happiness has nothing to do with the day. It has everything to do with your evaluation.

Myth Number 6: Make My Day

Movie buffs are familiar with famous lines like Vivian Leigh's, "I shall never be hungry again." Or Lauren Bacall's, "All you have to do is whistle." And there is Clint Eastwood's terse, threatening, "Go ahead, make my day." Although weird, and the line involved the thought, "Make the wrong move, and I'll blow you away with my .357 Magnum," it indicated that the death of a thug would have made "Dirty Harry" Callahan happy to kill a criminal. Sadistic, yes. Bizarre, indeed—but the scenario gave the viewer the notion that another person's misstep could lead to a policeman's happiness. To make it plain, what another person did would cause Callahan's happiness.

This myth proposes that other people and circumstances are responsible for our happiness, which is not the case at all. We are living in an age when we transfer blame to others, whether our spouses, our fellow employees, our bosses, or other significant others. All too often if people are not happy, they blame another person. Many a marriage crumbles because one or both of the spouses are totally depending on their mate to provide them with day-by-day happiness and joy.

It is easy to fall into the trap of this myth because it is basic human nature to hope to locate happiness in the lives of others. "If only my husband (or wife) would do thus and so, then I could be happy." "If my boss were more understanding, then I could have fulfillment." "If my kids would only respond as they should and please me, then it would make my day, my week, my month, and maybe even my year."

Why must we always depend on others to make us happy? That is not the key. Others may help to make you happy, but ultimately it is left up to you. You! If you want a guarantee of happiness, you must go ahead and make your own day. Haven't we lived long enough to realize that others will eventually let us down and disappoint us? Decide at the outset of every new day: "I will make my own day, whether or not others help me."

Myth Number 7: Paradise and Perfection

Now, admittedly this is a complicated, tricky psychological ploy. This myth goes like this: in order to be very happy I need to find either a paradise outside myself or perfection within myself. Many perfectionists have fallen prey to this myth. They ruminate, "The only way I can be happy is to have everything just right — all my ducks in a row, everything hunkie dorie."

There are no Heavens, Utopias, or Nirvanas here, no paradise on earth. Face it. This "vale of tears" can be a cruel, monstrous, hideous abode. All you have to do is watch the televison, listen to the radio, or read the magazines and newspapers.

Perfectionists are never genuinely happy because they expect more of themselves and existence than is possible. No matter how hard they strive, they will always end up asking themselves, in the words of Peggy Lee's song, "Is that all there is, my friend?"

If you believe this myth, you'll never, no never, be happy—because, as I have already explained, you will never have it exactly right, just so, either within society or within yourself.

Myth Number 8: High Way to Happiness

This myth became prevalent in the 1960s and continues until this day. It teaches: Substances like alcohol or other drugs are a viable means of experiencing happiness. However, attempting to escape reality is never the answer but only proliferates one's problems.

Momentarily, drugs or alcohol may put you "out of your mind" and cause you to feel less miserable for a brief period, but they will not and cannot make you happy. Perhaps you may remonstrate, "Now, really, Steve, very few of us fall into 'The High Way to Happiness Theory,'" but all known statistics contradict your argument.

Many, many people are dependent on the crutches of drugs and other substances to carry them through the day and the night. Nicotine and caffeine often are used as jump-starts. More people than we realize fall back on momentary stimulants that end up being depressants. They feel that their happiness depends on tobacco, however used, a cup, a glass, or a bottle.

No doubt you have heard your friends and associates comment, "Wow, I just can't get started in the morning without several cups of coffee and a few smokes!" And many have also bought into this myth

37

by overeating because it seems to give them "a high." Sometimes they joke about it: "I don't eat to live—I live to eat." Whenever a person overindulges and does not exercise moderation, he has crossed the line into myth number 8.

Myth Number 9: Ruined Happiness

This is a pernicious myth like all the rest. In essence, this mistaken notion declares that one person, by himself or herself, without doing any physical harm, can destroy the happiness of another person. You may well have heard somebody accuse another with, "You've ruined my happiness." Since your ultimate happiness is up to you, if your happiness is ruined, *you* are the culprit. You did it yourself.

This myth is kin to The Make-My-Day Theory. Actually, it is the converse of that myth. Since you are responsible for making me happy, if you have not done that, you have ruined the happiness I might have enjoyed. You and I must learn to laugh at such falsehood.

The indisputable fact is: you can have happiness within your life, come hail or high water. But you must want it, and you must lay aside all of these myths and rationalizations.

Myth Number 10: The Money Myth

This errant notion is that money will buy and secure our happiness. Have you ever noticed that people who have no idea what they want out of life feel sure that whatever it is, money will provide it for them?

They mistakenly believe that if they could only stumble into a huge financial windfall, the lottery, The Publisher's Clearing House Sweepstakes, "The Fairy Godmother," the demise of the legendary and sometimes unknown "rich uncle," that suddenly everything would be copacetic. That is simply not true. Mounds of money do not constitute a lifetime cure-all. It cannot guarantee happiness.

As I mentioned before, plenty of money may make misery a bit more tolerable, but then again many rich people aren't even happy . Reality is that beyond a certain point, added wealth cannot significantly improve the opulence of your life-style or increase your pleasure.

Is there a substantive, practical difference in life-styles between living in a 100-room mansion, a 200-room mansion, or living in a ten-room domicile? Besides bragging rights, how does unused floor space improve the quality of someone's life? Actually, many people who are desiring greater wealth are unaware that what they really yearn for is an increase in self-respect, security, power, freedom, and love.

I doubt if they actually want stacks of green paper to count. What they yearn for is the positive inner feeling they erroneously believe huge sums of money will give them. Unfortunately, money doesn't always work to produce those longed-for feelings. It's true sometimes that maybe a new Mercedes might give one that "click-your-heels" feeling. Designer clothes, running with the socially "in" crowd, and spending monstrous sums to become a member of the "jet set" and the "cruise set" may sound fabulous. Yet, it all boils down to this—money also may produce destructive, negative emotions if we let it, depending on how we look at wealth. Some people respond to wealth with worry and greed, anxiety, jealousy, selfishness, arrogance, frustration, and a lack of self-confidence.

Mindrobics Techniques for Dispelling These Myths

The first technique is:

1. *Enjoy life.* Merely make up your mind that you're going to be happy. You might reply, "How corny! You mean just to go ahead and enjoy life, no matter what happens, come what may?" Precisely. Happy people by and large are those who have made a definite decision to be happy and not to dance to the discordant rhythm of those ten myths.

2. *Make yourself responsible for your own happiness.* That's definitely not original with me. I picked it up from Plato, the ancient Greek philosopher, who mused, "The man who makes everything that leads to happiness depend upon himself and not on other men, has adopted the very best plan for living happily." The crucial core is to accept that responsibility for happiness in your own self and not grope around trying to force other people to make you happy.

3. *Constantly realize that you were put here to enjoy life.* From a human standpoint the Russian novelist Leo Tolstoy, though a literary success, had more than enough to make him unhappy, but he rose above his circumstances. (I collect quotations about happiness from sources around the world. In your own life you can build happiness by reading the works of happy people. Make their thoughts a part of your reasoning processes.)

Count Tolstoy wrote, "I believe that life must and can be a constant joy, and the wise person is always joyful." How can one have happiness in life? How crystal-clear it is. The way to enjoy your life is to understand that you're given life to enjoy. If you're not enjoying it, examine why not. Study yourself. Find out where you've made the mistake.

For three straight Sundays the new minister preached to his congregation on the subject of "repentance." After the third sermon on repentance, the church board called him aside and, rather disturbed, asked him, "How come you keep preaching on repentance? We mean, enough is enough! This is three straight sermons on repentance. Don't you have anything else?"

The minister replied, "When you repent, I'll quit preaching on it!"

Maybe your response to my counsel is, "Look, we've heard all that again and again." All right, when will you act on it? We have heard that "advice is cheap." Perhaps it is, but this is good, solid advice. It starts with the assumption that life is meant to be enjoyed. Many people who dwell in never-never land believe that happiness is not intended to be.

Yet Tolstoy starts with the foundation that life is given us to be enjoyed. We're here to have fun, to enjoy ourselves, to be happy. Then the Russian sage suggested that if you're not happy, if happiness isn't the norm for your life, instead of beating yourself up and condemning yourself, discover what's wrong.

4. *Observe happy people.* If you're not happy as you pass through your life, instead of merely feeling bad, begin to inquire of yourself, "What can I do differently? What are happy people doing?" and start to observe them.

This is one of the most beneficial strategies that helps us to engineer our happiness. Seek out happy people. Cross their paths. Watch them. Listen to them. Talk with them. If possible, be brazen enough to inquire, "What's your secret to being so happy, so full of life?" If they're genuinely happy, and not putting on a front, they won't rebuff you or turn you off. More than likely they'll try to give you an answer. Why? Because genuinely happy people want other people to be happy, too. Greedy, selfish persons will put on the facade of happiness for their own purposes. Their responses to such a question as "What's your secret?" will belie their inward unhappiness.

40

Yes, there are a few happy people around. I do hope you were able to think of at least one or two or five or even ten as you launched into this book. Think of that person or persons. Visualize them. In your mind get a feel of them.

When I used to view happy people, I would think, "Well, they were just born blessed. They're just happy by nature." But the more I've come to know truly happy and positive folks, I've found that many of them have encountered unspeakably horrific problems. They have often struggled; they have had to overcome innumerable setbacks; many of them were born with two-and-a-half strikes against them. They weren't necessarily raised to be happy.

Plenty of happy people were raised by hateful, spiteful parents, but these happy people have not wasted their potential by blaming misfortune on their environment and heredity. Happiness is not caused by environment and heredity but rather by that inner self-directedness that determines, "I'm going to be happy regardless of my environment or heredity."

What really motivated me to pursue the concept of happiness? Maybe you're talking to yourself, "Yeah, it's easy for him to speak of happiness because he probably hasn't had those problems. Man, he probably came up with a silver spoon in his mouth. When he refers to problems, he's probably just making a joke." No, sincerely I have many, many problems, and a few years ago I had one that almost devastated me.

I was thirty-three years old and had never been married, always wanted to be married, and finally did. And from almost day one my marriage turned out to be a disaster. It was a dreadfully negative experience. It blew a hole in all my dreams and desires. It was hellaciously tough, and I remember shortly into that marriage thinking, "If I'm going to count on another person to make me happy, and if I'm going to expect totally pleasant circumstances to make me happy, then I am condemning myself to misery for the rest of my life."

Instead of continuing to cater my own pity party, I kept on thinking. Sometimes that's not easy to do. We'd rather our emotions run wild with us. Emotions in themselves are not bad, of course, but we have to wed them with logic and reason. Many a person who lived out his emotions is either in the ground or in prison.

41

There are those, called "masochists" in the psychiatric literature, who love wretchedness and pain. I do not believe the Psychiatrist of the Universe wants any of us to wallow in hurt and misfortune. So I had a conversation with myself. My conclusion? I don't want to be miserable. Some people enjoy it—but not Steve Simms. Then my mental computer kicked in with an a most logical question, "What can I do?"

From that moment I began digging for these Mindrobics ideas and techniques. In this book we have only begun. Many exciting and effective techniques are within these pages. Happy people are not merely "blessed," born with a bent toward happiness. Lay aside all preconceived notions and let's walk into the following chapter and zoom in on what happy people do ...

Some people change jobs, spouses, and friends, but never think of changing themselves.

— Paula Giddings

The whole world will change toward you when you change your attitude toward it.

— Orison Swett Marden

Most people want to change the world to improve their lives. What a wasted effort. If they would only improve themselves, they would be better off and so would the world.

— Gerhard Gschwandtner

6
AT THE KEYBOARD
OF YOUR MIND

THERE IS A CHANCE that one out of four readers play the piano, but I certainly don't. If you do play, regardless of your skill level, I want to use piano-playing to summarize the principles I have covered to this point.

Life Is a Piano

I like to think of life as a piano. If I sat down and tried to play the piano, it would hurt your ears. Suppose you do play; you enter a concert hall, sit down and play Bach, Brahms, or Rachmaninoff, and there is tumultuous applause and a standing ovation.

Then you exit the stage as I enter behind you. Years ago I did learn to play "Chopsticks" and could pick out the melodies of one or two songs. I'm pretty talented, aren't I? So, let's further suppose I sit down to play after your magnificent performance. I try my all-thumbs hands at "Chopsticks" and "When the Saints Go Marching In." Naturally,

I screw up, and the audience begins to boo, hiss, and throw rotten fruit at me.

What's the difference between those two situations? Is there the slightest difference in the piano? No, the piano's the same—a Steinway, a Yamaha, a whatever. You and I have played the selfsame instrument, but the difference is: you were performing with a style and grace that produced harmony, melody, and exquisite beauty. At the same time I was, with all the aplomb of an inebriated chimpanzee, coming out with chaos, discord, and noise. It's not the piano's fault but how we're playing it.

This is an apt analogy of life. Some people enter life, and they emit lovely sounds. They're the happy people we want to emulate and imitate. They indeed "make beautiful music" with their lives. They enjoy life. In turn, they serve as catalysts for elation and joy.

Others, like all of us, come into the world screaming. But the trouble is: they continue to scream and make nothing but noise all through life. They may sometimes wind up in prison and/or down and out (and, yes, there are those who are the "ups and outs"). Their lives are tragedies. Willie Loman of the award-winning play, *The Death of a Salesman*, serves as a quintessential example. Most of us pass through life, and we're neither remarkable successes nor splendid, happy human beings. Most of us are not profoundly miserable, but we're not that happy either. We're sort of in between, in an emotional limbo. We're the bland leading the bland.

Write this on your shirt cuff, on your blouse, on a napkin, on the table cloth, or even on a pad: The key is—it's not life. It's how we play it! I stumbled onto this poem:

> Life itself can't give you joy
> Unless you really will it.
> Life just gives you time and space
> It's up to you to fill it.

Your life and your emotional, mental, and spiritual capacities are basically like most everybody else's. All human beings, unless they have major medical problems, have almost the same size brains and the same number of grey-matter cells. We also have the same types of nervous systems.

Even as there are various types of pianos, they are still essentially the same, unless they are damaged or out of tune. A skilled pianist can play most any piano—if it is normal—and do creditably. If it's a broken piano, the greatest pianist may not do exceptionally well. If it's in tune and repaired, the piano will sound good beneath the talented hands of a piano virtuoso.

I could play the best concert piano in the world and make it sound lousy without working hard at it! And that's how it is with life. Most of us have the basics—the brain, the nervous system, what one writer called "a bag of tools." But many often abuse and misuse those God-given tools, playing gross disharmonies, harming not only themselves but those in contact with them. How do you play your piano—or guitar or autoharp or zither or violin—fiddle, if you prefer?

Happy Habits and Behaviors

Through application and research I have discovered, plainly and simply, certain approaches or strategies of happy people—things happy people do. Happy folks have developed habits or behaviors that make for their happiness and further their happiness through all sorts of ups and downs, ins and outs, highs and lows.

Choose Happy Thoughts

That's one of those behaviors. Happy people deliberately concentrate on positive, uplifting, triumphant, good thoughts. A spiritual sage advised, "As a man thinketh, so is he." Genuinely happy women and men are at the keyboard and are effectively playing their own minds.

Before proceeding I throw in this quote: "If happiness consisted of physical ease and freedom from care, then the happiest individual would be neither a man nor a woman. It would be an American dairy cow." So there's hope for the rest of us!

I repeat: happy people opt for happy thoughts. They do not live in the pits and "the slough of despond." Through the centuries philosophers and theologians have argued over the influence of "mind over matter." It's according to how you slice it.

Certain religions and philosophies teach that one's thoughts can directly change the impersonal, physical world. Parapsychologists like Uri Geller even claim to bend silverware merely with their thoughts. I have seen Geller and others on TV, and they are rather convincing. However, scientifically verifiable evidence that thoughts alone can change non-living matter is virtually non-existent. Whatever "evidence" exists is shaky at best. And most people think tricks are involved in most so-called phenomena.

But even if your thoughts can't change inanimate objects, your thinking can drastically change you. Thoughts can change your attitudes, your abilities, and your health. Dale Carnegie spelled it out:

> As a result of thirty-five years spent in teaching adults, I know men and women can banish worry, fear, and various kinds of illnesses and can transform their lives by changing their thoughts. I know, I know, I know. I have seen incredible transformations performed hundreds of times and I have seen them so often that I no longer wonder at them.

Carnegie is still renowned for his Dale Carnegie Institute he founded in the early 1930s. He wrote a number of best-selling books, including one that is still in print after almost sixty years, *How to Win Friends and Influence People.* There is no doubt that he has influenced four generations of inspirational-motivational speakers and authors. He was convinced that changing your thoughts can dramatically change your life.

Thought control, not money or love or friends or "good luck," is a key. If you're not controlling your own thought patterns, then either someone or something else is, or you are totally out of control, an accident waiting to happen.

The Futility of Controlling Circumstances

All of us, at one time or another, have tried frantically to control our circumstances. As I have already emphasized, one can never totally control his outside world. You may have an unblemished driving record, and then—wham—another driver runs a red light or a stop sign, and you are in the hospital. You did all within your power to drive defensively, correctly, and legally, yet you had no control over an irresponsible driver.

In this world this or that is always going wrong. The only place you can exercise full control in your existence is within the arena of your own mind. We have heard and read about hostages in Vietnam, Iran, Iraq, and Lebanon. The ones who survived came through by the sheer power of controlling their minds. Commander Ralph C. Gaither was in North Vietnamese prison camps, including the notorious "Hanoi Hilton," for seven years and eight months. All that kept him and his mates going, even though they were separated from one another in pits and so-called "tiger cages" and tortured almost constantly, was the thought: "By God's grace, by a higher power, we are coming through this. No matter what they do to our bodies, they cannot kill our minds and spirits, even by brainwashing."

Yet, innumerable people who have never experienced such grotesque privation have already surrendered control of their minds. They have somehow inwardly determined there is no point in trying to live a meaningful life, that life is a drag, and so they are merely going through the motions. Their thoughts bounce aimlessly around, ricocheting off of the outward conditions of their world. No wonder they feel so bad.

Your Attitude Is a Mind Matter

Happiness and attitude comprise an "inside job." Nail it down: Happiness does not depend on outside occurrences, but on inward intents. It's not what happens to you, as we saw in the "The Three E's of Encouragement." It's how you respond to what happens, how you deal with matters.

People are always wanting to "work things out." OK, go ahead and try to work things out, but have you noticed that precious few people are willing to work things *in*? We want to "grab the bull by the horns" toward our outward circumstances, and sometimes the "bull" gores us. Why not grapple with the inward beast and harness our own thinking? I cannot statistically prove it, but I believe that most people spend more time trying to balance their check books than they do working on the tally sheet of their own thoughts. They consume hefty chunks of valuable time in trying to fight against all those "bad things" in their lives. And in all too many lives, matchless human potential for joy, peace, love, and other wonderful, affirming emotions, is surrendered to a life of unnecessary frustration.

*We give up troubled feelings only as we come to know
that the more painful way of life is not to give them up.*

— Lucy Freeman

*You will succeed best when you put the restless, anxious
side of affairs out of mind, and allow the restful side to
live in your thoughts.*

— Margaret Stone

*Fear is not a wall but an emotion. And like all emotions
it can be overcome.*

–Gwen Goldsby Grant

7

UNDERSTANDING
FEAR AND ANXIETY

THIS CHAPTER NATURALLY FLOWS from the previous one
on controlling your mind. I confess it's awfully difficult to control
your thinking. For instance, certain psychologists conducted a rather
sadistic experiment on a tomcat. Why they chose a cat, I'll never
know. They starved the cat for several days, only giving him water.
Then they carried him into their laboratory and set before that starving
cat a heaping bowl of the best cat food money could buy.

Maybe you have already caught the point. The cat tore into the
food like a hog gobbling down slop. The psychologists were not
surprised because they had more in store for that poor feline.

For the next phase of their experiment, they rudely interrupted the
cat's dinner, hooking him up to a fluoroscope. They weren't content
merely to watch the cat eat. They wanted to observe what was going
on inside of the cat as he was eating. The fluoroscope showed that
the food was moving on down. As the cat was eating, of course the

food was going down his esophagus and into his stomach. His "systems were go."

Here was the catch. The psychologists opened the door to the laboratory and let in a mean dog that immediately snarled and growled at the cat. Then entered Fear versus Hunger. That's a dilemma for a starving cat—or anybody for that matter. Of course, he was aware of his canine nemesis. The cat arched his back, laid back his ears, stiffened his legs, extended his claws, and locked his eyes on the dog— but he kept on eating.

Even though the cat continued to eat and all looked relatively the same on the outside, the psychologists noticed through the fluoroscope a considerable change. As the cat was stuffing food into his mouth, the stuff stopped moving into its stomach. His internal system literally shut down because of fear.

Lessons from the Tomcat

If a few moments of tension can do that to a hungry cat, can literally stop his digestive system, think what a continual attitude of unhappiness can do to a human being. In our culture, no wonder we buy so many over-the-counter and prescription drugs. We attempt to fix the symptoms of this unhappiness without diagnosing the real problem—the misery we're feeling.

Legitimate and Illegitimate Emotions

One approach that could help you and me to overcome unhappiness is: Begin to recognize the difference between our legitimate negative emotions, like the fear the cat felt—he had every reason to feel threatened and scared—and our destructive negative emotions. I refer to the anxieties we have in day-to-day life. There are extremely important differences between these types of emotions. If only we can learn to differentiate, it can mean the difference between abject misery and absolute mirth.

The Difference Between Fear and Anxiety

General Dwight D. Eisenhower, the account goes, was walking among his troops on June 5, 1944, prior to the Normandy Invasion of World War II. He was a five-star general and the leader of perhaps the most effective attack force in the history of warfare. He encountered a young private who was almost in tears, and the general

50

invited, "Son, let's walk a while"—a "General of the Army" strolling along with a private.

Like a caring father the general inquired, "Son, what's on your mind?" The soldier replied, "General, I'm nervous. In fact, Sir, I'm scared. I don't want to be scared, Sir."

General of the Army Eisenhower nodded his head, patted the private on the back, and answered, "So am I, Son, so am I. I'm scared, too." What a general!

Every honest human being has fears. Sometimes we have the mistaken notion that fear is always bad, always negative. Not so. Sometimes fear is a positive and necessary emotion. Eisenhower and the anonymous buck private had reasons for fear. Oftentimes we have reasons, too. The Bible records that "with fear Noah prepared the ark." Fear can be helpful and therapeutic. Anxiety, however, is always destructive and negative. And yet, many people don't quite recognize the difference between those two emotions.

Fear is a biological response to a present, real danger. It serves a practical purpose by preparing the body for a fight or flight. In response to fear, adrenalin flows into the bloodstream, increasing the body's speed, energy, and strength. Our veins and arteries are constricted in order to slow bleeding in case we are wounded. The pulse quickens, and the bodily defenses stiffen. That is the function of fear.

Anxiety, though, is not a response to a present, real danger. Instead, it is a pre-response to anticipated or possible future danger. There's nothing real when we feel anxiety. For years I have heard, "We worry about 1,001 things that never happen." Anxiety is that queasy, sickening emotion within that whispers to us, "Something disastrous and monstrous is just around the corner." Anxiety causes us to focus negatively on the future and all it portends. And untold multitudes die, not because of actual dire circumstances or events, but because of fretful anxiety that leads to hypertension, ulcers, colitis, cardiovascular disease, and emotional and mental illness. Considering the facts, anxiety, I repeat, is a poor response to anticipated danger.

Clutch Instead of Brakes

Here's another example. If your vehicle's brakes go out, what you feel is fear. Who wouldn't, especially if you're headed down a hill.

I remember the time I hit a deer on a mountain in Northern California. The deer hit my windshield and literally sailed over it, whiting it out. I was going down a steep grade. I hit the brake, and it was not grabbing. It was dead, and I was afraid I soon would be too—dead. You'd better believe I was scared. I was barreling down that mountain, couldn't see through my windshield, and had no brakes. Then I looked down. I had my foot on the clutch instead of the brake! I don't think I'd ever qualify for a semi or bus driver and certainly not for NASCAR. I immediately stopped the pick-up, but, of course I was feeling fear.

Fear normally subsides when the confrontation or mishap is over, when the danger has ceased to exist. After I was able to stop my pick-up truck, pull over to the side, and climb out for a breather, my fear had disappeared. I was no longer afraid because I was out of danger.

Contrasts

For instance, anxiety is what you sense if you're worried about an upcoming test in school, a job evaluation at work, or, in my case, what I am going to do when I speak to a professional group or company in two or three days. Yes, I start to worry—well, maybe not worry, but to be overly concerned. I can become somewhat uptight. Once in a while a feeling of dread drops in, and I ask, "Now, suppose you have a mental block. Suppose you bomb and they never want to hear your voice or see your face again?"

That's anxiety. Anxiety goes on and on, but fear stops when the danger is gone. Its purpose has been accomplished. Fantastic, you're safe, you're alive, you're out of danger. Fear is no longer necessary.

But anxiety goes on and on and on. Don't you hate it? It often becomes an emotional habit and devours a person's mental and physical well-being for years. Now we might as well admit it. Our culture is anxiety-inducing. Quite frankly, the more other cultures copy us, the more ridden with anxiety they become. In order to draw a paycheck, if one is fortunate enough to have a job these days, there are usually pressures of workloads, deadlines, quotas, and schedules. The worse the economy, too, the worse the pressures. Many people are afraid not to become workaholics. More and more workers are staying at their work stations even for breaks and lunch. Unfortunately, many of us have become habituated to anxiety.

Instead of confronting and dealing with that habit of anxiety, what we often do is try to tranquilize with various substances, hoping to follow "The High Way to Happiness" myth.

Because life is uncertain, and possible future dangers do lurk over the hill, there's always a reason for anxiety—that is, for those who choose to find one. I could begin picking out negatives about my life right now and what I'm facing today, tomorrow, and in the future. Oh, yeah, I could work myself into a lather, projecting all of the gremlins and goonies out there plotting to wreak havoc in my life and cave me in. Nope, but I'd just as soon not find a reason for anxiety.

Non-medical Prescriptions for Anxiety

Many who would rather avoid anxiety have discovered an ancient remedy in a quote. It sets forth a highly effective technique. It happens to be from the Bible: "Do not worry about tomorrow for tomorrow will worry about itself. Each day has enough trouble of its own." Fear deals with today's troubles. Anxiety and worry try to grapple with tomorrow's troubles.

When you're in actual danger, your fear helps you to protect yourself. Happy people, through controlling their thinking, learn to avoid anxiety at all costs—or certainly to minimize it. When you can't fight or you can't flee, then go with the flow. If you're in a situation and you can do something about it, you can fight it or run from it—fear's appropriate. If you can neither fight it nor run from it, then at least do your best to avoid anxiety.

Plato observed, in essence, "Nothing in human life is worth very much anxiety." There is a wise attitude, and remember that Plato was taught by Socrates, and Plato in turn discipled Aristotle, who is considered the founder of modern Western thought. But it's not always easy to avoid anxiety.

We all run into those who talk a good game but don't live it. It's easy to lecture others and then for the lecturer not to heed his own advice. Soothsayers are all around us, chanting, "Well, don't worry." "Don't worry, be happy." And that's to take nothing away from Bobby McFerrin's number-one hit of several years ago. It's just not that easy.

In spite of our best efforts, there are times when we all experience a sneak attack of anxiety. You seem to be doing A-OK . . . and all of a sudden a wave of blind terror sweeps over you, and you have no idea why. You may think sirens sound, your ears may ring, sanity shakes, chills of apprehension frigidly engulf your mind. You are going through a panic attack of anxiety that launches an internal avalanche of dank, dark, negative thoughts and emotions. Is there a defense against such a dreadful onslaught? Well, here are some ideas that may help you.

Conquering Anxiety Attacks

The key to avoiding anxiety attacks and dealing with them if they occur involves five simple steps. All of these relate to your thinking and how you use your mind efficiently and wisely.

1. *Realize that anxiety attacks will come.* Everyone with mental and emotional faculties is attacked by anxiety. My Dad has a plaque on his office wall. It bears the quotation: "Be kind for everyone you meet is fighting a tremendous battle." That is one of our points of commonality as human beings. From time to time—let's hope not often—anxious thoughts will enter our minds. Accept them as being normal. Like them or not, they are a part of living. Anxiety is not choosy. It attacks young and old, rich and poor, people of all races, creeds, and backgrounds. So, friends, don't be surprised when it picks on you. It's no big deal. You can cope with it as routine. It might even help to use that old quote, "This, too, shall pass."

2. *Continually build and prepare a strong mental and emotional defense system by becoming an avid positive thinker.* Hopefully, that's what this book is helping you to do: to erect in your mind a fortress of life-giving, positive thoughts and emotions. Hey, I hate to pull the plug out of your bathtub, but even happy, positive people are attacked by anxiety moments. The difference is that positive people don't give in to anxiety. Positive people have inwardly fortified themselves with affirmative emotions and thoughts to the extent that, when the negatives rear their heads to disrupt them, they can effectively ward off anxiety attacks. As a source of life-giving, positive thoughts, I recommend the Bible or a Bible-promise book.

3. *Be always on your guard and ready for a surprise attack.* Don't go around in paranoia, looking over your shoulder for anxiety, because that would aggravate a condition conducive to anxiety, but you are never aware when anxiety will sneak up on you. Yet, prepare to nip anxiety in its bitter bud. A tad of anxiety is far easier to repel than a full-scale attack. I've found that when anxiety thoughts begin

bombarding me, if I can deal with and vanquish them as soon as they start, it's infinitely easier to overcome them than entertaining them for a day or even a week or two.

Some anxious souls have petted and stroked anxiety thoughts for half a century, and it will require tremendous effort to dispel negative thoughts that have embedded themselves and festered for a lengthy period. But it can and will be done if you follow these techniques for three weeks and make it a habit, even second nature. It's simply far easier to deal with anxiety in the beginning. Once you have allowed anxiety to overwhelm you in a particular situation, there's really very little you can do in that situation except ride out its fury. But then, prepare yourself for the next attack and keep a guard posted in your heart.

4. *When anxiety attacks arise against you, fight them with all your might and power.* Slay them with your emotions and thoughts, positive actions, and a confident posture. Winston Churchill, voted by *Time* magazine the outstanding personality of 1900-1950, was often beset by depression he referred as "a little black dog that nips at my heels." He was familiar with attacks of anxiety, but his advice is worth noting, "Never, never, never give up."

5. *Always remember that your fight against personal anxiety is a high and noble cause.* We often hear of armies going to war, fighting to defend their countries and contending for freedom and liberty—but it's fully as noble to fight against the inward negative thoughts of your mind for your own personal sanity and happiness. Emily Dickinson penned these lines:

> To fight aloud is very brave,
> But gallanter I know
> Who charge within the bosom,
> The cavalry of woe.

Anxiety is an insidious and potent foe. Your war could last for years. Personally, I still fight anxiety, but the fight well fought, with a passion to win, will dispel your inner enemies in the end.

It is better to look where you are going than to see where you have been.

—Florence Griffith-Joyner

The future belongs to those who believe in the beauty of their dreams.

—Eleanor Roosevelt

Worry is an old man with bended head carrying a load of feathers he thinks are lead.

—Corrie ten Boom

8

ANTICIPATION, NOT ANXIETY

DO YOU REMEMBER the TV commercial about ketchup (or catsup, however you spell it) where the camera zoomed in on an inverted ketchup bottle. As the ketchup started to ooze slowly onto a steak, the melodious voice of Carly Simon was singing her hit "Anticipation" one syllable at a time—"AN-TIC-I-PA-TION."

Reliable old *Webster's Dictionary* defines anticipation as "a realization beforehand," and anticipation is thrilling. It's the eager and enthusiastic expectation of positive experiences in your life.

There are two kinds of insomnia—anxious and anticipatory. Many creative people are so excited about the exhilarating prospects of the following day that sometimes it is difficult for them to sleep. With elation they sometimes lie awake, writing books and articles and composing music and planning business strategies in their heads. They can hardly wait to jump out of bed and give it a go once again. Anticipation. But then there are those who toss and turn, conjuring up the specters of tomorrow, anxious over the slightest assignment that awaits them at work. They are not only anxious over "things that go bump in the night" but also things that might "go bump" in the day. They are continually going through a nocturnal hell.

Anxiety Versus Anticipation

Starting each day with anticipation is indescribably marvelous. Why not ask yourself, "What good things are going to happen today?" So many overwrought, burned-out people are thinking, "Well, I wonder what bad things are going to happen today?" Anticipation helps us to be happy, enthusiastic, and brimming with joy. As a person anticipates a new day, he feels like a child with an amazing new toy. William Carey, the British missioner, was the founder of the Protestant modern mission movement. He launched evangelical missions advance around the world with this unadorned phrase, "Expect great things from God. Attempt great things for God." Expect great things for every day. Anticipation transforms thoughts of the future from dread to decisiveness.

Anxiety's Mate—Apprehension

Sadly, though, many of us face the future with anxiety or apprehension. Apprehension is defined as the dread or fear of future trouble. Of course, our helter-skelter society does nothing to discourage apprehension. For example, if you browse most any book store, you will discover stacks of books about impending doom, about the crumbling economy, about seemingly insoluble problems all around the world. The fact is, I am aware of people who no longer enter book stores—and even those who never read newspapers or magazines or watch television or listen to the radio. Somehow they are trying to insulate and isolate themselves from the world, even though they are still, as it were, going out into the workplace. The shelves are laden with negative books. It seems that often the majority of newspaper stories feature the worst possible events of the day. The same is true with radio and television. It almost seems the media is pandering to its viewers' and readers' dark sides. On major TV networks within one week recently there were interviews with three confessed killers who seemed to love every minute of exposure. At least three prime-time TV shows and probably four books have come out about a now-glamorized teenage girl who confessedly shot and paralyzed her alleged lover's wife. The girl is now virtually lionized—even glorified.

"Tomorrow, Tomorrow, Tomorrow"

Is it any wonder that many people live with apprehension to the degree they become what I call "dreadheads," always expecting bad things to happen to them and filling themselves with anxiety and tension. The so-called "psychic" hotlines are making money hand over fist because people want answers about their anxiety and apprehension. Imagine paying up to $5 per minute to have a distant, unknown "psychic" supposedly provide answers for the future concerning money, love, family matters, jobs, and conditions in general!

No human being honestly can know the future beforehand, whether it's going to be good or bad, so doesn't it make sense to expect the best instead of the worst? Isn't anticipation a more enjoyable attitude than apprehension? Think about how children anticipate Christmas, birthdays, and other holidays. Have you ever seen such joy as revealed in little children as they anticipate those gifts that Santa has in store for them?

Since anticipation produces such a positive outlook and bubbly joy, why not choose to look toward the future with anticipation instead of apprehension and pent-up anxiety? Why not make a deliberate choice to anticipate? Hope for, pray for, except the good. You may comment, "What if the future still turns out bad? What if I anticipate the good things, and they don't happen?"

In that case at least you've made the present moment more enjoyable by avoiding apprehension. Even if you anticipate something good and it doesn't come about, anyhow you've enjoyed looking forward to the expected good. Jesus advised us to "Take no thought for tomorrow ... ." What did He mean? Not that we never consider tomorrow. That's not it. Newer translations state, "Don't worry about tomorrow." That's the clue.

Control Your Worry and Your Thoughts

One essential if we are to achieve happy thinking is to realize that happy people control not only their thoughts but also have charge of worry. They learn to cut down on worry and to rid themselves of it. One alternative to worry is that "positive people" think about the good things they want. There is no reason why you cannot do that, too. In that process you will banish thoughts of what you don't want.

Anticipation, Not Avoidance

The Illustration of the Golfer

To me a classic example of this is the predicament of a golfer who reaches a huge water hazard, maybe even a lake, smack dab in the middle of the fairway. The golfer, whether a duffer or a pro, may think to himself, "I'm not going to hit the ball into the water, not going to …." So he swings and … kerplop. The ball sinks into the lake. This is not magic or legerdemain. This illustrates a mental reality: if you expect to fail, if you visualize that ball going into the water, if you think about a situation you don't want, you're unconsciously causing your mind actually to aim for that.

So, instead of thinking, "I want to avoid this," anticipation dictates, "I want to achieve this. I want to hit the green and make a par or even a birdie." Dread declares, "I'm not going to hit into the lake," but anticipation asserts, "I'm going to hit it right to the green." So how does one move from dread or apprehension to the triumphant feeling of anticipation?

The Illustration of the Tree-planter

Another idea is similar to planting a tree. Most people have planted at least one tree — or certainly a plant. It's not automatic when you plant a tree. You simply can't toss the tree out into the yard and command it, "Grow, tree, grow." No way! I've almost tried that, and the tree dries up and dies, pronto. It requires considerable work to plant a tree and then nurture it to maturity. First, you have to dig the hole, and that means persistence and repetition, maybe moving shovel after shovel of dirt. It may become boring and tedious, but you must do it if you want that tree to grow.

Then you have to set the tree properly in the hole. And then there follows adding dirt and fertilizer. You're still not finished. It sounds tiresome even to think about it. If it doesn't rain nearly every day, then you must regularly water the tree. Eventually it may need to be shaped or pruned and sprayed for insects. When you plant a tree, you have to care for it over a period of years if you really want a healthy tree. Then, decades from now you can show it to your grandchildren and maybe even your great-grandchildren. Even then, after all that hard work and care, your tree may still die. Then you have to dig it up and start all over.

Maybe you've figured I don't plant too many trees. You're correct. Why? Because it's too much work. Besides, one tree, more or less, in my yard is not going to make much difference in the quality of my life anyway. Frankly, if I'm going to work that hard, I'd rather plant positive thoughts in my mind and yours. And that's really far more difficult than planting a tree!

Greenville Kleiser, an author in the early part of this century, mused, "Your thought is the builder of your body, the molder of your character, and the ruler of your destiny." What a heavy statement! Good thoughts, planted firmly in your mind and constantly nurtured, will make a dynamic difference in your life.

Good Thoughts Require TLC

I can recall when folks would prepare fried chicken by putting the chicken pieces, along with salt, spices, and flour, into a paper bag—and then shake the bag vigorously. Then they would place the chicken pieces into a sizzling skillet. But you can't merely toss a positive thought into your mind and expect it to live. It would be half-baked or half-fried. The thought would neither be cooked nor grown.

Do not kid yourself. To plant positive thoughts into the fertile soil of your gray matter, intensive and extensive work is called for. "TLC" means "tender, loving care," and you must lavish your positive thoughts with it. Remember that those thoughts are precious and priceless. You may briefly latch onto an excellent concept, file it into your mental computer, and then inadvertently press your mind's delete button.

First of all, you must use persistence and repetition, repeating a thought to yourself over and over, maybe hundreds of times a day. Then, you must be mentally tough and evict the negative thoughts that want to destroy your tender, new thought. The weeds of anxiety, apprehension, and unfounded fears will converge in a malevolent effort to negate your positive idea or thought. We will have to resist all those negative forces and keep working at it until the new, positive thought becomes automatic.

Greenville Kleiser also noted:

> Start a single thought in your own mind, and with proper nourishment it will grow and multiply into innumerable useful thoughts. The ideas you repeat frequently enough ultimately acquire undisputed authority over your life.

Thoughts have power; thoughts are energy. And you can make your world or break it by your own thinking.

— Susan Taylor

The happiness of your life depends on the character of your thoughts.

— Marcus Aurelius

Attitude is the mind's paintbruch. It can color a situation gloomy or cheerful. In fact, attitudes are more important than facts.

— Mary Crowley

9

HAPPINESS PRINCIPLES THAT MAKE SENSE

W HY HAVE I REMAINED on the characteristics of positive persons? And why have I emphasized that truly happy people select thoughts that make them happy? Because all of this goes straight to the core of happiness.

Now I move from my previous illustrations to happiness principles.

Ralph Waldo Emerson, one of America's most famous essayists, stated, "Thought is the seed of action."

C. N. Bovee, not so famous, however, expressed it well: "The pleasantest thing in the world is pleasant thoughts, and the great art in life is to have as many of them as possible."

I have already established that nothing is perfect in this life and that none of us are complete and 100 percent emotionally, mentally, and spiritually mature. But by staying at the steering wheel of our thoughts, we can have more satisfying control of our lives.

It shouldn't even be necessary for me to write this, but thoughts are the spring of action. You will spring in the direction your thoughts are coiled. In other words, people either develop mental muscles or mental misery.

It's this plain and unvarnished: Either you learn to control your thinking—and in so doing rid yourself of tormenting thoughts and infuse your mind with therapeutic thoughts—or you will cohabit with life-long anguish and misery.

Who, Me, Worry?

The late William E. Gaines founded the satirical magazine *Mad* with a cartoon representative named Alfred E. Neuman. His motto was "Who, me, worry?" The implication was Alfred was dumb, but he didn't worry. This is sensitive, but I will spell it out. It is actually dumb to worry. Worry is a pain in the gluteus maximi. Worry is unfruitful and unprofitable.

Worry is a troublesome, negative thought pattern. I have heard it referred to as "the beating of the mind against the walls of darkness." Worry is an enormous waste of time since the mind is not focused but consumed with anxiety, flitting from here to there and seeking light in every conceivable direction.

Worry emotionally, mentally, physically, you name it, literally wears a person down as the mind becomes depleted of energy—going nowhere and accomplishing nothing. Worry is essentially disorganized thinking. Liken it to blights, plagues, toxins, and every conceivable evil, and you will have summed up worry. So why do we continue to worry? Why not do away with it? Why not declare a moratorium? The only antidote for worry is intelligent, controlled thinking.

What Will It Be?

Believe it or not, life normally becomes what we expect it to be and what we believe it will be. It surely would help us to remember that our minds are not rusty filing cabinets or what we used to call "chests of drawers," a place where we can throw odds and ends. And it is not only a storehouse to file away information. It is a divinely given endowment for our use. Your brain, consisting of millions of cells, is the most sophisticated computer of all. You can program your mind, even as programmers work out programs for PCs and mainframes.

Helen Keller, one of the most remarkable persons in history, was blind, deaf, and mute from an early age. In spite of her seemingly insurmountable adversities, she wrote, "I have found life so beautiful." Her positive philosophy of life, including control of her thoughts, was one of her keys to a happy life. She further said, "I've learned that it's possible to create light and sound and order within us, no matter what calamity may befall us in the outer world."

The Origin of Positive Thoughts

Positive thoughts are not the result of happiness. So many people believe that, once you "get happy," then you'll think positive thoughts. Nope. Happiness springs from positive thoughts. Before we experience happiness we must make a practice of thinking positive thoughts. High-level performance is always the result of that sort of thinking. Basically this is a matter of discipline, of assuming control.

Martin Luther, the reformer from whom the Lutheran Church is named, expressed it in these words, "A thought is like a bird. You can't stop it from flying across your mind, but you don't have to let it build a nest there."

The Power of Thoughts

Thoughts are immensely powerful. Some people remark, "Well, that's just mere thought," or, "It's only a thought, so it doesn't matter." But speaking of mere thoughts is about like speaking of mere dynamite. Andrew Carnegie, the industrialist (not related to Dale), believed in the power of sheer thought to the point he declared, "The person who acquires the ability to take full possession of his own mind, may take possession of everything else to which he is justly entitled."

Dale Carnegie, whom I quoted before, said, "I know with a conviction beyond all doubt that the biggest problem you and I have to deal with, in fact, almost the only problem we have to deal with, is choosing right thoughts." You see, we are not finally hurt by what happens to us. We're wounded by our perception of what happens to us.

Mark Twain, one of the cleverest authors in American literature, in talking about thinking, wrote, "Life does not consist mainly, or even largely, in facts and happenings. It consists of the storm of thoughts that is forever blowing through a person's head."

There are even medical and scientific reasons that decidedly demonstrate why thinking is vastly important to us. Thoughts are the commanders of the brain. They are impulses that trigger electrical and chemical switches in the brain. The brain is not simply a thinking organ but is also the largest secreting gland in the body. When given an electrical command, which is a thought, the brain sends chemicals coursing through the body. These chemicals are called BMDs—"brain-made drugs." They're what psychologists call psychochemicals.

There are two types of psychochemicals that can be released into and are continually turned loose into your brain. These are stressors and endorphins. Stressors are negative chemicals that, of course, cause stress within your body. They make your gastrointestinal system tight and upset; they cause your blood pressure to accelerate, your hands to perspire, your entire system to respond with feelings of anxiety, dread, and off-beat emotions.

The other type of chemicals your brain emits into your body are called endorphins. Endorphins, according to Paul Pearsall, the author of the book, *Super Joy*, are 200 times more powerful than morphine. Endorphins provide us a natural high. You've probably had that on-a-roll feeling, where you've had a sense of satisfaction and fulfillment, and you feel you could conquer the world. Those feelings are precipitated by the endorphins.

You have seen grandparents literally glow as they have talked about their grandchildren. You have encountered people who are hopelessly in love. Or you have run into a friend who had a significant raise or promotion. The endorphins are flowing copiously!

Maybe you or your friends are sports fans, and you had a team you were really rooting for. Suppose they won the Super Bowl or an NCAA Tournament or a National Championship. When they won, you felt fantastic. When they put that game or tournament on ice with that final score, didn't it send chills up and down your spine? That feeling doesn't come from the score, because, if you'll notice, the opposing team and their fans don't cheer. If the score gave the feeling, the other team and fans would cheer, but the feeling actually emanates from thinking about it.

As you think those good thoughts, endorphins—those drugs from your brain that elate you—are released. On the other hand, when you concentrate on negative thoughts, those lousy negative stressors run amok in your system and pull you down. After a fan's team loses, and, with downcast eyes, he shakes his head and moans, "Oh, I'm just sick at my stomach," he may literally mean it. The stressors are making his body unhealthy.

So by literally controlling your thinking, you can also rule over your feelings, because you can help command what types of chemicals your brain secretes.

All right, then, what can we do about that ...?

It is the nature of thought to find its way into action.
— C. N. Bovee

The stronger and better your thoughts, the stronger and better will be the results of your daily efforts.
— Greenville Kleiser

There are gems of inspiring thought which we all can use. You must search for them.
— Ethel Waters

10

HARNESS YOUR THOUGHTS

W HAT CAN WE DO about our thoughts? How can we harness them so the endorphins will predominate over the stressors? Pick and choose as you please, but here I offer ...

Techniques for Controlling Your Thoughts

The first technique for controlling your thoughts is: *Don't editorialize*. What do I mean? Have you noticed more and more how daily newspapers, in so-called news stories, tend to express opinions rather than reporting the facts. It seems that has spilled over into our lives. Many of us want to make value judgments about everybody and everything.

If this or that happens to you or another person, don't comment. Don't make it good or bad. Try to deal only with the facts. As Joe Friday of an earlier generation tersely said, "Just the facts, Ma'am." Marcus Aurelius well illustrated that point: "Say nothing more to yourself than what first appearances report."

Let's suppose you have heard that someone has been saying bad things about you. Remember, this has only been reported. But that you have been injured, that has not been reported. In other words, if

69

you hear about a person bad-mouthing you, say, "Well, I heard this person's talking about me," but don't expand on it with, "And he's ruined my reputation, and things are really awful," because then you'd be editorializing. Happy people control their thinking by just dealing with facts, and they don't add to those facts.

Another positive technique is to: *Saturate your mind with positive material* (which I trust you're doing as you're reading this book). I have covered this before, but it bears repeating.

Another technique may sound strange, but it is: *Practice do-it-yourself brainwashing.* All of us are going through processes of brainwashing. Because of certain psychological atrocities during World War II, the Korean War, and the Vietnam War, we tend to think of all brainwashing as negative. Not so. If you don't wash your own brain, somebody else will! So start taking charge and feeding your brain what you want it to know and follow.

Here is another potent technique. You may not be able to help how you feel at this moment, but you can certainly help the way you think and act about your situation. When matters are not going well, instead of giving in to them, tell yourself that you are in control of what you think. You may not be able to stop what is happening, but you can think about it however you please.

For peace of mind, resign as CEO of the Universe. Quit fretting about situations over which you have no control—hot spots around the world, hurricanes, earthquakes, floods, massive starvation, "faraway places with strange-sounding names." Let your worries go. Concern yourself only with what you can control and help to improve or change. Now that ushers in a certain amount of peace, doesn't it?

This bears reemphasis: Counteract negative emotions and thoughts with positive ones. And when those negative thoughts surge in your mind, replace them with the positives, the good, the uplifting ones. When you are faced with a challenge or task, you may think, "I can't do that." Knock that in the head with, "Oh, yeah, I can, and here's why!"

Another great technique is: *Live in the present with your thinking.* When an unpleasant thought resurrects itself from yesterday to hound you, here's a straightforward rebuttal: Yesterday ended last night.

No doubt you have answered me throughout these pages, sometimes with, "Well, Steve, what about all these maxims and slogans? Do they really do any good?" Yeah, they do when you apply them. They're like tools—a hammer or saw, for instance. A hammer won't do you any good sitting on the shelf. It won't drive a nail unless you pick it up and swing it. Neither will a saw cut a board if you leave it lying in your tool shed. Use those instruments, and they'll work. That's doubly true with these techniques of positivism.

Another approach that has proven helpful throughout history is: *The card-carrying technique.* It consists of writing positive, triumphant ideas and thoughts on cards and carrying them around with you. Also surround yourself with positive-thinking posters. Put your cards on your desk or office bulletin board, on your bathroom mirror, on the dashboard of your car.

I repeat this one on purpose, and that is to: *Mind your media.* This is exceedingly important in this age of gloom-and-doom media reports. Many people are blue and depressed because they wallow in bad news. Monitor what you read, hear, and watch. I am not suggesting that you flee from reality but that you manage your intake. Rule out the crass, crude, and grisly aspects from your media consumption. Bypass the tabloids that major on the S's—sensationalism, scandal, and sex. So what, even if Prince Charles did tell his lady friend, "I want to get into your trousers (or knickers)"? Life is too short to devote your precious time to such thoughts.

This technique also bears repeating: Lighten your lingo. Do not put yourself down. Others are more than happy to do that for you. Try going easy on yourself. Talk to yourself positively, instead of negatively. Ethel Waters is often quoted as commenting, "God don't make no junk." Actually, her quip was, "God don't sponsor no flops." Remember that. You were, to use the Transactional Analysis book title, *Born to Win.*

Another technique I have found supportive is: *The Thought Stopper.* Like Martin Luther observed, "Those thoughts will come." Underline this—you may not be able to stop them from visiting your mind, but you don't have to let them build a hotel there. When a bad mental impulse trots onto the stage, direct it to exit quickly. Demand that it move on. And do that right then and there!

Consciously resist a dark, depressing thought. In fact, command it, "Get out of here. I resist you. I am not going to think along these lines." It is a proven fact that your mind cannot think two thoughts at the same time, so if a bad thought is en route, run it out of town before it reaches Main Street. "No, I will not think this. Stop, stop,

71

stop." That will disrupt a bad thought and keep it from gaining access to your mind.

Express happiness is another strategy for building happy attitudes and thinking. The entire process works in both directions—express happiness and, in turn, think happiness. How can you demonstrate or express happiness? Think it. Talk it. Live it. Maybe you remember the cartoon "Li'l Abner" that died when Al Capp, its creator, did. Among its characters was a "Ziggy" type of hillbilly, Joe Bflfx (or a similar jumble of letters), who walked around with a black rain cloud always hovering over his head. Will you glow or be like Joe, always depressed, dismal, and downtrodden? If you want to glow, determine to express happiness.

Don't Fall Asleep at the Wheel

Letting your thought processes frolic unattended is similar to falling asleep at the steering wheel—or either driving a vehicle, removing your hands from the wheel, and hollering, "Whoopee, look, Ma, no hands!" If you fall asleep at the wheel or withdraw your hands, you may end up dead or severely injured. By the same token, if you take your hands off the steering wheel of your mind, you'll find yourself in deep trouble, without honestly wanting to be where you end up. So, it's not a bad idea to decide where you want to go and what you want to do with your life. Or does it matter?

A businessman was on the road and spent the night at a hotel. He arose in the morning ready to head for home, so he checked out of the hotel and ate breakfast at a restaurant next door. As he walked outside, it was raining, and he reached for his umbrella. "Oh no," he moaned, "I forgot my umbrella. I better go get it." It wasn't in the restaurant. No one had seen it.

He then thought, "I bet I left it in my room." As he approached the room he thought again, "Maybe I can get there before the maid does. I left the door open, so maybe I can get my umbrella before anyone else checks into the room." As he came toward the room, he noticed the door was closed. He was sort of discouraged but kept on going. He thought a third time, "Well, that's not too bad."

As he reached the room, he heard voices inside, and the first voice was male, asking, "Whose little feet are these?" And a female voice answered giddily, "They're yours."

And then the male voice continued, "Whose little legs are these?" The female voice replied, giggling, "They're yours."

The questioning kept on with the male voice inquiring, "Whose little thighs are these?"

About that time, the businessman outside the door could stand it no longer. He banged on the door and yelled, "When you get to the umbrella, that's mine!"

Of course, you're asking, "What has this got to do with thinking?" Didn't the businessman have to control his thinking not to let his mind go bonkers over what he heard through the door? He was focused and intent: he wanted his umbrella. That funny story illustrates three principles of success.

Pivotal Principles of Success

First, happy people know what they want. The man wanted his umbrella. As he was leaving, he controlled his thinking. Even though he forgot (common to us all), he didn't become all frustrated, raving and ranting and red in the face. He zeroed in on the umbrella. That's what positive and happy people do. They know what they want. The businessman kept his thinking straight.

Second, happy people take action to gain what they want. That man set out to retrieve his umbrella.

Third, happy people are not distracted from their aims and goals. Negative agendas and attitudes connive to sidetrack us from gaining what we desire. Nothing is accomplished by spending one's time trifling with "can'ts" and "won'ts." Our umbrella man could have listened in and become frustrated, or to the opposite extreme he could have gotten vicarious kicks with the male-female interchange. He did neither. He stuck with his purpose, "I want my umbrella. I need my umbrella. I'm going to get my umbrella." He harnessed his mind, kept it under his command. I once heard the counsel: "Watch out where your mind tiptoes when your back is turned." Happy people keep a close watch on their minds.

Laugh and the world laughs with you. Cry and you get all wet.

—Anonymous

It is pleasing to God whenever you rejoice or laugh from the bottom of your heart.

—Martin Luther

Laughter is an instant vacation.

—Milton Berle

11

ENJOY YOURSELF WHILE YOU'RE AT IT

Most people like to be around upbeat, positive fellow workers and acquaintances. If you laugh for the right reasons, others will gravitate to you. If you're always moaning the blues, they will tend to avoid you.

Laugh, and the World Laughs with You

Appropriate laughter is indescribably healing, soothing, and re-creating. Laughter will even help you to keep your thinking straight. How? When you start taking yourself too seriously, nothing is better than to lean back and laugh—not necessarily at others—but at yourself. Have you ever noticed that no one who laughs healthily seems to fall into serious trouble when they're laughing? That's because laughing people are enjoying themselves too much to court trouble.

A hearty laugh, not at someone else's expense, is like sunshine, warming the soul. Chamfort wrote, "The most utterly lost of all days are the days in which you've not laughed once." So laugh every time

75

you feel tickled, and laugh every now and then just for the sheer fun of it.

When a person throws his head back and belts out a belly laugh, depression, negative thoughts, and painful emotions flee. Laughter shakes down the foundations of hurt and sadness, clearing the way for the spontaneous eruption of inner joy. Addison put it: "Laughter breaks the gloom which is apt to depress the mind." And Stern said, "I am persuaded that every time a man smiles, but much more when he laughs, it adds something to his life."

Laughing sets off biological processes that improve a person's health and make him feel good. Laughing increases the blood flow to the brain and the oxygen level in the arteries and veins. It relieves stress and tension. I have already mentioned endorphins. Yes, laughter releases those valuable endorphins into the body—those brain-made drugs that create a "natural high."

Most people wait for laughter to sneak up on them from behind the drone of dull, daily existence. A few people, though, keep on the lookout for humor, staying alert for the slightest reason to break into laughter.

The other day I had an extra-good laugh. I became creative with my dishwasher since I was out of my regular dishwashing detergent, so I decided to substitute liquid dishwashing stuff. I thought, Well, they're both for the same purpose—to wash dishes. But my dishwasher didn't appreciate my originality. It began to protest by oozing out suds. There were enough suds to furnish Cleopatra's baths for a millennium. The suds began to flood my kitchen floor like a congruent army. But I didn't let those suds conquer my kitchen or my attitude. I found a bath towel and engaged in hand-to-suds combat. As I began to fight the suds, though, for some strange reason, I didn't notice the natural humor of the situation.

All sorts of negative thoughts bubbled and floated in my mind. There I was about to be swept away in a maelstrom of detergent suds. After all, this is on the value of laughter. So I called my mental reserves and engaged in thought-to-thought combat with those negative old intruders. I flexed my mental muscles. I imagined myself out of body, looking down on the situation, and I pretended it was happening to Lucille Ball, and I burst into convulsive laughter. What a hilarious sight! I wish you could have enjoyed it with me. An ocean of suds and me trying to clean them up. And what an episode of *I Love Lucy* it would have made.

We human beings are funny creatures. The "funny video" shows are not essential. If one looks for funny experiences, every day is crowned with the comedy of life. Too often we miss the humor of the moment, because we're too embarrassed, too "sophisticated," or too anxious merely to lean back and laugh.

The first lesson to learn is to laugh at ourselves. You're the best comedian you'll ever meet. You. Rather than playing the role of a tragic actor and thinking all those bad thoughts, why not occasionally enjoy being a clown? That's one problem today. With so many special-interest groups, nearly all of them are becoming up-tight. Throw your head back and roar. Now I'm not saying make a joke of your life. Not at all. I'm just saying your life already is a joke. Just ask people who know you. You'll find they have been seeing humor in your life for years. Why not join them and have a good laugh at *yourself?*

Laugh for Your Health's Sake

There are medical and scientific reasons to laugh. According to Dr. Lars Ljungdahl, the director of Primary Health Care Center in Motala, Sweden, "The lack of a laugh may be hazardous to your health." Dr. Ljungdahl, with his laugh therapy, has demonstrated that laughter suppresses the hormones that cause stress and that laughter actually reduces pain.

Ljungdahl believes his research is universally applicable. He says, "The people of Motala, Sweden, have a reputation of complaining, so if laugh therapy will work with them, it will work anywhere." Ljungdahl's goal is helping people give a higher priority to humor in everyday life. He concludes, "Jokes are fine, but the humorous events of everyday life are better medicine."

He meets with his patients for thirteen weeks, reviewing comic books, comedy records, and humorous videos. For homework, Ljungdahl asks his patients to keep records of funny happenings they observe. Then, they rank them on a one to five scale from barely funny to hilarious. Dr. Ljungdahl's patients have experienced a reduction in their levels of pain, an improvement in their immune systems and in the overall quality of their lives.

American researchers agree with Dr. Ljungdahl. Gail Wilson, a Chicago-based humor consultant, said, "Laughter is a great stress reliever." And Lola Gillabrand, a Southern California humor therapist, stated, "When we laugh, we automatically feel better."

Returning to Dr. Ljungdahl—he further noted, "The humor perspective is a way of getting distance from your problems. Since every person has a sense of humor and every child laughs, it's not so much learning something new as it is regaining what you once had."

The key to recovering your humor perspective is concentration, thoughtfulness, and playfulness. Locate a quiet, restful place to begin and vividly remember something outrageously funny—a story, a person, an experience. Visualize such in your mind. Fantasize. Pretend you're a knight in King Arthur's court, "Sir Laughalot."

And laugh and laugh and laugh. Yuck it up unashamedly. And you'll release those positive little fellows, the endorphins, and they'll cavort and romp all through your system. You'll feel better ... and your thinking will be better, too.

Still having trouble loosening up and laughing? W. C. Fields once said, "Everything's funny if it happens to somebody else."

If you slip on a banana peel, that's serious business. If someone else slips on a banana peel, that's humor. Next time you slip on one of life's banana peels, why not pretend it's happening to someone else? Pretend it's someone else who is stuck in traffic, or missing a plane, or overflowing the toilet, or whatever. A simple change in perspective will often release a flow in your life!

Belief in yourself is the prerequisite for health and happiness.

— Dr. Arnold Fox, M.D.

It is difficult to make a man miserable while he feels he is worthy of himself and claims kinship to the great God who made him.

— Abraham Lincoln

A human being can stand a lot as long as he can stand himself.

— Alex Munthe

12

SEVEN WAYS TO LIKE YOURSELF BETTER

HOW DO YOU FEEL if and when you have listened to negative comments and put-downs all day long? Worn out, right?

Since all of us are flawed persons, it's easy to find something wrong with anybody and everybody. Too thin. Too fat. Speaks too softly. Speaks too loudly. Has a bad hairstyle. Does this. Doesn't do that.

Yet, what about going through every day looking for the good instead of the bad? Are you aware that sometimes an inefficient employee is like that because all they hear is criticism and never commendation. You can find something you like about most everybody. Why not try pointing it out to them?

You don't have to comment, "Gosh, you're the best-looking person I've ever seen in my life." That's a bit much. If it's the first person you've seen that day, you can honestly say, though, "You're the best-looking person I've seen all day," because that's true and sincere. Paying sincere compliments can make you feel better about yourself and life in general.

Try the Smile Factor

Maybe you haven't complimented anyone in a while. Why not? Are you living only for yourself? Maybe you've forgotten how good it is to make other people feel upbeat about themselves. So I challenge you to make five people smile in an hour. Isn't that far better than making them frown? The more you truthfully compliment people, the happier they and you will be.

Dr. Theodore Rubin gave this advice for depressed people: "Choose a friend, who at the moment, is in greater emotional need than you are, dedicate yourself to him or her for the day, even though it may take considerable effort. Try to cheer him or her up. Use your total energy, however depleted you may feel, for this person's well-being and for making him or her feel better."

This idea can be very helpful in overcoming the blues. Dedicate yourself to it. After you've complimented people, if you're still blue, find somebody that needs you, and dedicate a whole day to helping somebody. It will help to refocus your mind away from your own problems.

Dedication to Making Others Happy

It's like the paradoxical teachings of the Bible: "If you lose your life, you'll find it." "If you give you will get in good measure." "If you die to your own selfish wishes, you will gain for eternity." This is the principle. If you "lose" yourself helping someone, you will discover that you will find yourself, your true self, because you will become happier than you were when you were trying to locate happiness directly.

If we pursue uplifting others, happiness will be a by-product. Before we are fully aware of it, we will be "surprised by joy," to quote C. S. Lewis' book title.

Mary Kay Ash, the founder of Mary Kay Cosmetics, defined this principle: "Whenever I meet someone, I try to imagine him wearing an invisible sign that says, 'make me feel important.' I respond to this sign immediately and it works wonders." Every person you meet has that kind of sign. If you are sensitive to that sign, they will respond to you and treat you well ... and you'll feel good.

You yourself will have happiness as you create an atmosphere of happiness for others. A Hindu proverb goes, "Help your brother's boat across the river and lo, your boat also will have reached the other shore." If you can forget about pursuing your own happiness, and help someone else to reach happiness across the river, before long you'll be happy too. Happy people cause happiness wherever they go. Of course, unhappy people cause unhappiness. Since they are miserable, they live by the old axiom, "Misery loves company."

A poem by M. S. Bridges illustrates this:

> Life is the mirror of king and slave
> 'Tis just what we say and do
> Give to the world the best that you have
> And the best will come back to you.

Would you believe that certain people might comment, "Well, I just don't feel secure about making other people happy"? We must remember that the foundation of making other people happy is to like yourself. It sounds almost contradictory, but you cannot love others until you love yourself. Without concern for yourself you cannot have genuine concern for others.

It is a strange person who does not enjoy hearing the words, "I like you." But all too often people want to hear that phrase but not to express it themselves. That reflects nothing but self-seeking and self-centeredness. So if you can learn to like yourself, it will make it easy for you to compliment other people. Phyllis Diller said, "If someone doesn't like himself, it's almost impossible for others to like him."

Seven Principles That Work

These are tried and true Mindrobics techniques that have worked for me and many others. These principles will help you to think about others after you begin to like yourself.

1. *Don't compare yourself with others.* You were designed to be yourself and nobody else. I feel the terms "normal" and "average" are deceptive and elusive. People are not the same. We're all different, as different as snowflakes and fingerprints. Rating yourself by other people's standards, opinions, and abilities will always make you come up short. You're always at your best when you're

comfortable being like whom? Yourself, that's who! One approach to liking yourself is: just don't compare. I'm not to be like you. You're not to be like me. I'm just me. You're you.

Years ago, when I started comparing myself with others, it was a bummer for me. A "jock" I'm not and never was, but I tried comparing myself to athletes. When I was a kid and they chose up sides for sandlot games, I still remember the lengthy arguments, "You take Simms. No, you take him. No, you take him. Well, we'll take him if we can have his last strike." Neither team wanted me. They wanted me to bat tenth on a nine-member baseball team.

For years I disliked myself because I lacked athletic prowess. Then I finally learned to quit comparing. It no longer mattered. Being athletic is not the standard of being a good person. Whatever you are, it's OK. Accept it. Just be you. Hey, you're not "one in a million." You're one in more than five billion!

2. *Stay in line with your conscience and your own moral standards.* I could violate your moral standards, and I could somehow live with it. In turn, you could violate my moral standards and still make it. I have definitely concluded this: If I violate my own moral standards and values, I feel guilty, sad, down and out. It's almost impossible to like yourself when you feel guilty. Guilt ferments when you think or do things that you personally believe to be wrong and unacceptable for you.

If you do things somebody else thinks are wrong, you won't feel guilty. But when you do, say, or think things you feel are wrong, guilt will pound on you and cut you down. So, to like yourself more, hammer out your own set of values and live them. Absolutely refuse to violate your own conscience. Go by your standards and hold them up. Yet, don't try to impose those on others, and you'll like yourself more.

3. *Forgive yourself.* Every one of us has broken our own principles. We've all blown it. That merely means you're human. You make mistakes, so acknowledge you were wrong. Correct your wrong behavior, and then learn from it and, once and for all, put it out of your mind. The past is gone. Now strive to be faithful to your values in the present and in the future.

I believe the majority of people violate this. They beat themselves up emotionally and mentally. They fall into a pattern of criticizing themselves and blaming themselves for the past. What a waste of human potential and resources! All that does is make a person dislike himself. When you spend most of your time downing yourself, you're not going to be much good to anybody else.

4. *Separate personal worth from performance.* So many cannot separate their personhood from their work. Remember, you're not your work. If you are what you do, then when you don't, you aren't. If I'm only my work as a speaker, then when I'm not speaking, I'm worthless. But you are not your work—you're not what you do.

Build your self-worth on your infinite value as a magnificently designed, intricately crafted human being. Your ultimate value arises from your being human, and you're a human being, not a human doing. You are a person.

Let's suppose you have two snow shovels. You shovel the snow from your driveway, and then you go next door and shovel your neighbor's driveway. You put the shovel back into your garage. Then a person comes to your door and requests, "I'd like to buy one of your two snow shovels. I hear you've got two." Which snow shovel would bring the most money? The one you used to do all that work or the one that simply stood there in the garage? Neither one. They both would be worth the same.

That's how we human beings are. Underline this in the tables of your mind. The one that has done more work—who has the fame and the glory—is not worth any more than the one who hasn't done it. When you base your self-worth on that, it's easy to like yourself. I'm worth what I am because I'm a human being.

5. *Accept compliments from others.* Not only do we need to give those compliments, we need to accept them when they come to us. Don't reply, in mock humility, "Well, it's really nothing." Someone may compliment you on a meal you prepared, and you might answer, "Well, if the veal hadn't been frozen, it would have tasted much better." Or they may comment, "Steve, what a good-looking suit." And I might answer, "Oh, I just got it over at the discount store."

Have you noticed how people often do that? Hear me. Don't do that anymore. When someone remarks, "Oh, that's a great suit," say, "Thank you." When they compliment you with, "What a wonderful meal you fixed," reply, "I appreciate that. Thank you very much." Accept those compliments and allow them to build you up.

I have heard that if you reject a compliment, you belie a desire to be complimented twice. If I come back with, "Oh, it's just a cheap tie I got somewhere," what I'm probably wanting you to do is respond with, "No, no, I really like that tie." Not only are you asking for a second compliment, but there is the chance you are wounding a person's feelings. Healthy human beings should have an outlet for making compliments to their fellows. The underlying innuendo may be, "You don't know what you're talking about. You're not really telling the truth. You're not sincere. What do you want out of me? What kind of deal is this? I don't like you that much, so I reject your attempt to make me feel better about myself." Do not turn away compliments. Thank people for them. "Thank you" is the best response. And then savor them—but don't gloat over them either.

Now this is not an ego trip. If people write me letters thanking me for a speech or presentation I put those in a book. From time to time I'll dig out that book of letters and read them, especially when I am allowing myself to become blue or negative. Of course, they pep me up. Sometimes when I don't like myself, it helps me to realize that at least other people like me.

6. *Give yourself compliments.* Instead of only complimenting everybody else, and smiling at five people in an hour, sometimes pat yourself on the back. Mark Twain said, "When I can't get a compliment from anyone else, I pay one to myself." It's all right to appreciate yourself, so compliment yourself often. After all, you do some things right. If you're alive and you're breathing, you're doing something right. Your body is a wonder, and you're doing certain things right merely to stay alive.

Every person should compliment themselves several times a day, not to the point of being egotistical, of course. I don't mean to imitate Muhammad Ali when he ran around hollering, "Hey, I'm the greatest!" But if you don't build up your self-image, you won't be able to build up other people's and spread happiness around. Pay yourself a compliment. In fact, you might stop reading for a minute right now and pay yourself three compliments. Think about it. It may be difficult, but think of three things you like about yourself and compliment yourself. Then go back to reading. Are you back? I hope you did that.

7. *Use the affirmation, "I like myself."* In one of his tapes Brian Tracy recommended that affirmative statement. I started doing that. Every night when I hit the sack I say "I like myself" about twenty-one times—and the following morning, about twenty-one times.

This technique is remarkable. I used to have such an inferiority complex, and just by convincing myself, "Steve, I like you," I honestly do like myself now. No, not to the point where I think I'm better than anyone else, but to the plateau where I think I'm as good as anyone else. So I don't mind complimenting other people. Why? Because I don't feel competitive with others.

People who are afraid to give credit where it is due, are reluctant to praise others and to compliment them, have an identity crisis. Down inside they are fearful that others may look good or advance or obtain a pay raise or gain attention from the boss.

Maybe there's a lump in your throat—or you are even inwardly embarrassed—but say to yourself, "I like myself." Do that in the morning and at night. Repeat it during the day. When you're alone say it aloud. Say it until you lose track of the count. And then one day, you'll fully believe it, and you'll act on it. People who like themselves can effectively help others. Do you think Mother Teresa hates herself?

I hope you like yourself, but if you have trouble doing that, these seven steps, if followed for a year, will make you your own best friend

Monitor and Control Your Self-Speak

Another aspect of liking yourself is how you talk to yourself. Perhaps you've heard that only "crazy people" talk to themselves. That misconception is crazy in itself. All of us talk to ourselves. Let me ask you this: If someone you know talked to you exactly as you talk to yourself in your mind when no one else is listening, would you put up with it? Most people have trouble accepting abuse from others. If a friend or a neighbor criticized you, or if a stranger put you down, you'd more than likely come back with, "Hey, wait a minute. Don't talk to me like that. That's not right, and I completely disagree."

Yet, when it comes to talking about themselves and to themselves, many people let loose with a stream of invective that would make the toughest drill sergeant turn tail and run. Too many of us put ourselves down in attitudes and thoughts. I used to run myself down continually. Millions of people secretly despise themselves.

Maxwell Maltz, author of the book *Psychocybernetics,* estimates that 95 percent of all people have at least mild feelings of inferiority. Because of this, people often focus on the very best in others while

85

noticing only the worst in themselves. They view their rivals, their friends, and their neighbors as super humans, but they perceive themselves as poor examples of the human race.

In both evaluations they're wrong. As I have made manifestly clear, there are no super people. Successful people and happy people are just ordinary folks who have developed a strong belief in themselves and what they do. They've learned to speak positively and compassionately to themselves. They have learned how to compliment themselves realistically. So, how about you? Remember, self-dislike is far more than just a waste of time. It's a dreadfully important issue. If you don't like yourself, it lowers your morale, it saps your energy. It makes you physically sick, and it prevents you from taking constructive action. It keeps you from liking other people. If you don't like you, who else is going to? If you don't like you, whom you know reasonably well, how are you going to like other people?

Liking yourself is not talking about cockiness, machismo, conceit, or superego. Conceit means trying to convince other people you're important. Someone pointed out that conceit is the only disease that makes everybody sick but the one who has it! Conceit has been called "God's gift to little people." Conceit is not what I have in mind. Conceit is based on insecurity and a desperate need for approval.

I used to read that people who are real cocky and overly assertive are insecure, and it was hard to grasp, but that is the truth. People who really like themselves don't have to strut around like peacocks. They have no rationale for running other people down. They're open and honest, and they can encourage other people and still be happy while helping others to be happy. They don't have to wear a mask and make a masquerade of life. People who really like themselves are also able to enjoy the simple basics in life. They're able not to waste time and energy attacking themselves or others.

What we must have as human beings is self-belief. Self-belief is basically involved in the self-image. Instead of trying to convince others that you are important, if you are happy, you will work at convincing yourself that you're important—because you can make a difference. When you realize you are indeed important, the opinions of others will fade into oblivion.

People who accept and compliment themselves can live happily and successfully without the compliments of others, even though those compliments are beneficial. Not only that, they have the inner resources to spread the joy around and make other people happy.

Too few people live with zest or genuine enjoyment. They are regretting the errors of yesterday or worrying about the problems of tomorrow ... but the only moment you have to live is this one.

— Karin Roon

If you reach back to past successes, you reawaken confidence to succeed in the present. But if you go back to past failures, you defeat yourself.

— Maxwell Maltz

Regret is an appalling waste of energy. You can't build on it; it's only good for wallowing in.

— Katherine Mansfield

13

HAPPY PEOPLE REJECT MENTAL BLUESPRINTS

MAYBE YOU'RE ASKING, "What do you mean, bluesprints? I've heard of blueprints builders use for houses or other buildings, but mental bluesprints?" Transactional Analysis (TA) talked about "playing old tapes." Well, my term bluesprints refers to negative, painful memories we all have from time to time.

Bluesprints of failed relationships, the pain of golden opportunities—now gone—of what might have been, of shattered dreams, of innumerable hurts. Yes, you have them if you are human and have feelings. Remember when people hurt you, even so-called friends? Recall when he or she broke your heart a few years ago or maybe even yesterday? Reflect on when you were chewed out for practically nothing, when you were fired, when a "significant other," perhaps even a parent, pointed the finger and shouted, "You'll never amount to a hill of beans." Can you remember emotional, mental, and/or physical abuse—even from someone you loved?

Good grief, this complex world is running over with problems. It's a wonder any of us get out alive. The fact is, none of us do get out alive physically. Yet, many people will keep on recalling their bluesprints instead of leaving them dead and buried where they belong.

The Anatomy of Bluesprints

One of the worst bluesprints I used to have was over a college sweetheart. I still remember the day she told me good-bye. Actually, the words were closer to "get lost." I am not going into vivid detail because you probably can relate to this without elaboration. Whenever I was feeling blue I would pull out the bluesprint of that unrequited love. I would relive every painful moment of our relationship and her "get lost." I would throw myself a lavish pity party.

Then I would think maybe I was depressed because of my biorythyms. No way. It was my remembering the bluesprint. On Valentine's Day 1990 one of the Nashville papers had a collection of brokenhearted letters. Innocently, I began to read those letters—the first about a man whose wife had left him and how badly she had treated him (Yeah, I could definitely relate to that—I began to feel sad and sorry for the fellow); the second about a woman who had been mistreated by her boy friend (it was gruesome); and the third letter, the worst yet. It was so bad I don't even want to recall it. There were about twenty letters on that one page. The paper reported that its staff had collected those letters of tragic romances from Middle Tennessee over a period of six weeks. What a wonderful way to celebrate St. Valentine's Day!

When I read those letters, other peoples' misery and pain were depressing me. And if they can do that to you and me, think how bad your own hurt is! Those are examples of bluesprints. What I did with that article was cut it out and mount it on a posterboard. I would use it in speeches as an illustration of bluesprints, holding it up and explaining, "Many people feed on reading, seeing, and hearing material like this and cause themselves tremendous pain." Then one day in El Paso, Texas, I left it on the podium, and maybe a person on the night crew found it, read it, and came apart at the seams because of my forgetfulness.

Another example of blueprints is the classic movie, *Gone With the Wind.* That is considered one of the best movies of all time, and whenever I view it, I thoroughly enjoy it until the last ten minutes. That movie is rife with sorrow and tragedy, and it's difficult not to cry during those last ten minutes. Rhett and Scarlett are having troubles in their relationship, and he returns from Europe. She falls down the stairs and loses her baby. If that's not bad enough, their little daughter, whom they both love, falls off a horse and dies.

Then they decide to break up and end their marriage. And Mamie, the nanny, gets Melanie, their friend. The scene where Melanie and Mamie are walking up that staircase is heart-throbbing. Mamie, who loves Rhett and Scarlett, starts telling Melanie how bad it is and how they're almost ready to kill each other. Both Mamie and Melanie are boo hooing. Then Melanie goes home and dies. She's been in this movie for hours, and she dies, and I'm attached to her. And then, if that's not enough, "Frankly, my dear, I don't give a damn," Rhett snarls, and he leaves.

Then Scarlett, who is devastated and lying on the staircase, commiserates about all the sadness. But suddenly she says, "I can't think about it now. I'll think about it tomorrow." What an example of blueprints. The best advice I've ever heard for blueprints is to do what Scarlett did. When all these pains are piling up on you, don't dwell on them. Put them off. Think about it tomorrow. That's positive procrastination.

If It Hurts, Don't Touch It There

Maybe your child has come to you playing with a sore, almost crying, "Mom, Dad, everytime I touch it here, it hurts." You probably told him, "If it hurts, don't touch it there." And the soundest advice for blueprints is: if it hurts, don't touch it there! Avoid playing the painful memories from the past in your mind. Maxwell Maltz wrote, "The unhappiest of mortals is that man who insists upon reliving past pain over and over in his imagination, continually criticizing himself for past mistakes, condemning himself for his past sins."

Pain from the past can't hurt you unless you recall it into the present. Do your darnedest to forget past blues. Albert Schweitzer noted that "Happiness is nothing more than good health and a poor memory." Leave those bluesprints in the past. You may not be able to control the deposits in your memory bank, but you can control the withdrawals! Everything that happens to you goes into your memory, and there's nothing you can do to keep it from going in there.

Life is guaranteed to give you more than your share of unpleasant experiences. Because your mind is such an awesome computer, it will automatically store those bluesprints in your memory. For example, if you choose to do so at this moment, you perhaps can conjure up the memory of the ten worst experiences in your life.

Why would anyone want to resurrect their most disturbing memories? It only causes needless pain. Yet, all around us people daily torture themselves with painful memories. The bottom line? It's downright silly for people to employ their minds to make themselves depressed. The next step for many is an attempt to feel better by using alcohol and drugs and other diversions.

Stop! Wouldn't it be better if they didn't depress themselves in the first place? Surely every person has pleasant memories, not merely painful, and when you come down to it, it's really easier to remember a pleasant memory than a bluesprint. Once again, it's a matter of choice. You and no one else may pick the memories you call to mind. Are you being good to yourself by remembering your joys, your loving relationships, and your triumphs, or are you abusing yourself by dredging up your failures, your rejections, and your disappointments?

Buck Rogers, a former vice-president of IBM, confided, "I have what I consider a selective memory. I pick and choose which memories I'll draw from my memory bank, and I have chosen the memories that make me feel good." Happy people reject mental bluesprints.

Harold Russell lost both of his hands in World War II. Later he won two Academy Award "Oscars" as an actor and served as the national director of the Veteran's Administration. With a smile on his face, he often commented, "It's not what you've lost, but what you have left that counts."

The Mind—Camera-Computer

Watch a scene on a videotape with me for a moment. As we first glance at the screen it look like thousands of ants massed together in a ring. A closer look shows movement in the center. As the camera draws closer, it can't be. It appears the ants are playing football. The camera moves in somewhat closer, and it's not ants at all. It's a pro football game being viewed from a camera aboard the Goodyear blimp. The camera has a super-powerful zoom lens, and it can zoom in so close that you can make out tiny scratches on the players' helmets. I enjoy those shots from the blimp.

But you know what? You also have a "camera" of sorts in the "blimp" of your mind—that part of your mental capacity that towers above the rest of you. Your mental TV camera can picture a large image or a small one, even as the camera on the blimp.

Let's try an experiment. Close your eyes and picture the Empire State Building. Imagine it. Can you see it? Now increase the size in your mind. Make it ten times as large as any other building in the world. See it grow up. What a building!

Now reduce the Empire State Building in your mind back down to normal size—then shrink that awesome building all the way down to a two-inch toy. Tiny, isn't it? See a little boy holding the building in his hand, and then watch it diminish until it disappears, and there's no more Empire State Building.

Isn't the camera in your mind amazing? "What's the purpose of all this," you ask? Not a bad question. If you can envision the Empire State Building in your mind and make it ten times its normal size, can't you do the same with your blessings, successes, and good times? If you can mentally shrink the Empire State Building until it vanishes, can't you do the same with your bluesprints—those failures, fears, hurts, and problems that cloud your existence? Sure you can.

The only problem is that most people do exactly the opposite. They blow their bluesprints way up ten times their normal size and shrink their blessings down to tiny things. Instead, shrink the bluesprints, and make molehills out of the mountains of problems. And you'll definitely feel better.

Your Free Video Jukebox

Another example of bluesprints and how we deal with them is the video jukebox. I used to be fascinated with the old jukeboxes. Now they have jukeboxes that have video players above them. I know a place that has a free video jukebox. Doesn't cost a cent to play it. Not only that, it has the largest selection of any jukebox imaginable. This

93

free video jukebox has country, rock, jazz, pop, classical, big band, Gospel, anything you like. And all of the songs come with videos.

It's really amazing, this jukebox. It has songs and videos to put you in any mood you want. You can listen to songs that will make you happy or sad—you name it. There are scary songs in this jukebox, party songs, crying songs, laughing songs, love songs, hate songs, divorce songs. Select whatever songs you want to see and hear. Now because this jukebox is absolutely free, no strings attached, you'd expect the place to have a huge crowd. But just the opposite is true. There's never a crowd at this video jukebox. In fact, there's never more than one person there. That's because the place I'm talking about is your head, and the video jukebox is your mind.

By the time a person is twenty years old, he has several trillion images, sounds, and feelings recorded in his brain. That's quite a selection for a jukebox, and a person can replay whatever experiences he wants. Have you ever heard a song or seen a music video that made you feel good? You more than likely have. And have you heard a song or watched a music video that made you feel lonely, sad, or depressed? "I'll Never Fall in Love Again," "Bluer than Blue, Sadder than Sad," or "He Stopped Loving Her Today." They express profound emotions, but they are sad with a capital S. What you pay attention to changes your feelings.

I've eaten in restaurants that have jukeboxes or play music over their P.A. systems. I often am forced to hear cheating songs or broken-hearted songs. They're awfully depressing. But in my brain, I don't have to do that. In a restaurant, I may have to put up with those negative songs or either walk out without finishing my meal. But in my brain I can play what I jolly well please, and so can you.

Program Your Video Jukebox

If a person puts me down, I don't have to play a get-even song, a hate song, or a poor-me-why-did-he-do-that-to-me? song. No ma'am. Instead, I have several billion other tunes I can play. So when someone attacks me verbally, I flip through my mental Rolodex and pop out a "sticks and stones can break my bones but names can never hurt me" song, and in the background I play a breathtaking video of the Rocky Mountains. Then, instead of anger and ulcers, I experience peace and joy.

As long as I don't let somebody pop a sour song into my mental jukebox, they can't hurt me. Isn't that fantastic? No matter what they say, if I don't take those words and run a sad song, they can't hurt me. The words of other people can hurt me only when I use my mental video jukebox and run blue, sad songs. So why run pain, sorrow, and suffering bluesprints through your mind? Leave those CDs, tapes, whatever in the bottom of your jukebox. They can't hurt you down there. Don't play another "Somebody Done Somebody Wrong Song." Instead, punch up the good stuff, songs that make you feel fabulous, that set you to humming, that make you want to dance.

Play the songs about the time you won, about the time you heard "I love you," about the time you received a raise, about the time you were promoted, about the time your baby first cooed "Mama" or "Dada" ... about the "goodness and mercy" that have graced your life. What you play on your machine, you'll be. To change your feelings, change your inner song. If you want to feel great about a person or a situation, think good thoughts, refusing to play the bluesprints. I repeat: happy people reject them. Down-at-the-mouth, sad people play them all the time. Most of us play our tunes somewhere in between.

Anchor Your Own News

Personnel could change between now and the release of this book, but ... Dan Rather, Peter Jennings, Tom Brokaw, and other news anchors do the national news on TV. Most people watch these telecasts from time to time. Unfortunately, news is not always pure facts. When a newscaster presents a news report, he cannot completely turn off his opinions, his reactions, and his attitudes. One's opinion comes out somehow where human beings are concerned, even it is only minor.

For example, anything that happens can be reported from several angles. If there's a wreck, the camera could be put in different places. The newspersons could report what is good or what is bad about an event—or we might not hear about it at all. The decisions made about what and how to report the news—what to leave out, the camera angle, the slant, the commentary—all shadow the facts with people's opinions. So, no matter how sincere a reporter may be, another person may view the same story in a totally different light. Besides that, the TV networks must manipulate the news to make it fit thirty-minute time slots, minus commercials. No matter what happens that day, it takes exactly the same amount of time to report it. If there was a tremendous amount of news, they'd be limited to thirty minutes. If there was very little, they would handle it in thirty minutes.

Before we criticize the TV networks too much, what about the newsgathering and reporting organization in your mind? Consider how many million information bites your senses pick up every day. You cannot possibly keep up with all that is done and said around you and to you every day of your life. If you tried you might conceivably "blow a fuse." So it is absolutely essential that you select what you will report to yourself and what you will think about.

Unfortunately, many people, as they "anchor" the news desks of their minds, report to themselves only the bad input and play the videotapes of bluesprints—hurts, insults, arguments, failures, and worries. They accompany these bad-news bites with disaster-style negative commentary:

This news is sponsored by Bluesprints Builders and Gloom-and-Doom Tapes.

> Today I had car trouble and was five minutes late to work. Two of my fellow employees, Brenda and Judy, hardly smiled as I passed by. The bread for my pimento-cheese sandwich was stale. And, horror of horrors, one of my fingernails chipped. My stinking pay raise was only 3 percent instead of 5. It was terrible. Nothing good ever happens to me, Susie X. My life is virtually over. How can I survive? I'm ruined! What a miserable day and what a miserable life!

There are actually those who make a tragedy out of nothing worse than that report. How do I know? Because I have heard them lament about such out loud before their fellow workers. Yet, others choose to report the good. This does not mean they are Pollyannas living in "la-la land," but it surely does make them happy. For instance:

This news is sponsored by the Good News Company and the Be-Glad Video Store.

> My car broke down as I was driving to work. When I reported in, though, I breathed a sigh of relief and said, "Chief, I'm glad to be alive!" Two of my fellow workers were glum, so I complimented one, "Jennifer, I adore that dress." Jen brightened up right away. Ellen looked as if she had lost her last friend, so

I suggested we have lunch together, and we did. Now Jen and Ellen seem to feel better about everything. The "chief" called me in later on in the day and explained, "Janie, I consider you one of our outstanding employees, but you realize what we're going through right now. I wanted to give you a big raise, but it'll have to be 4 percent." I replied, "Chief, thanks. I'm grateful to be working with you and this company." As I close out this newscast I'm thankful to be alive, to have a job, to have a raise, to have friends, and more ...

Happy people run tapes of their successes, pleasures, hopes, and dreams. It's not even necessary to repeat that everybody has good and bad happen to them. The so-called "Lifestyles of the Rich and Famous" have plenty of bad. Believe it or not, some of the unhappiest people in the world are fabulously rich. More often than not they are tormented about never having enough, so they strive for bigger and better and more and more. They live in fear of being cheated out of their wealth, and they find it almost impossible to locate people whom they can trust. And to top it all, most of them are not sure exactly how much money they have.

Yet, "The Lifestyles of the Poor and Anonymous" are often brimming with happiness. Some of the happiest people I have ever known were poor folks. Honest. They weren't lazy. They were hard-working, they never complained, and they barely eked out a livelihood, but they were happy.

A friend of mine worked in a toy store while he was going to graduate school. He reported to me that possibly the unhappiest kid he had ever seen was not in the ghetto or in a shanty as a sharecropper's son. The totally dismal kid was escorted into the store by his personal chauffeur. For an hour my friend followed them throughout that store with thousands of items available. The boy either had it, it didn't suit his whims and fancies, or he was bored with it. After all that searching the rich kid left the store with nothing but the dissatisfaction and unhappiness with which he had entered.

The Clue—Anchoring Positively

What am I coming to? That wealth, social status, health, and other outward factors do not determine a person's happiness. No, the clue to happiness is how you and I anchor the news desks of our minds.

Yes, Steve Simms, the motivational-inspirational speaker and writer, has had more bluesprints than he cares to admit. How else could I help you cope with yours if I didn't have experience with mental bugaboos?

Several years ago I invested $4,000 in fire alarms. A powerful gent assured me, "Listen, you can make $30,000 a year part-time if you buy and then sell these fire alarms." I bit. I laid out the $4,000. You've already guessed it, haven't you? I never sold a fire alarm. I finally gave some of them away to my family for Christmas presents, and there are still quite a few in my basement. From the first moment I was leery of that man—had negative vibes about him. So, I built a bluesprint around him and the fire alarms. I kept whipping myself for investing that money when my incentive to sell did not match my money. In other words, I was not willing to put my motivation where my money was.

Sometimes these bluesprints will keep trying to torment you ... BUT I REPEAT. Reject them. Turn them away.

> Yes, you will make mistakes.
> Will you learn from those mistakes?
> Will you move on from them?
> Will you chalk them up to experience?
> Will you let them go?
> WILL YOU?

> I've shut the door on yesterday,
> and its sorrows and mistakes.
> I've locked within its gloomy walls
> past failures and heartaches.
> And now I've thrown the key away
> to seek another room.
> I'll furnish it with hope and smiles
> and every springtime bloom.
> No thought shall enter this abode
> that has a hint of pain.
> And every malice and distrust
> shall never therein reign.
> I've shut the door on yesterday

and thrown away the key.
Tomorrow holds no doubt for me,
since I have found today.

—Author Unknown

It doesn't matter what you've endured—separation, divorce, a disability, a so-called "handicap," the loss of a job, a drastic change in your job if you have one, and innumerable possibilities. Whatever has happened does not have to defeat the inward you—your spirit. Press on. Expect the good. If you believe in prayer, pray for the good, realizing that life is also tinctured with the bad.

Throughout this book I have emphasized that you must have charge of your mind in order to possess happiness. I have pointed out that you will never have personal freedom as long as you are bound by the shackles of destructive attitudes and thought patterns. Jesus taught His disciples, "Ye shall know the truth, and the truth shall make you free."

Truth is truth wherever you discover it. The principles of this chapter I have gathered from numerous persons and sources, known and unknown. Personally, I am a Christian, but that does not restrict me from gaining a certain amount of understanding from other philosophies and religions. The following five steps to happiness are from Gautama Buddha.

Restrain Yourself

Buddha's first key to personal freedom is to establish and maintain certain limits for yourself. The theologian Paul Tillich described the word "concupiscence" as "trying to take all of reality into oneself"—in other words, a grasping greediness to do, be, and have everything. No one can do that. Many of a person's natural desires are harmful and self-destructive. Harmful, hurtful emotions and attitudes cannot be removed without personal restraint and self-control.

We have enjoyed considerable mobility because of gasoline. In your lifetime you may have driven more than a million miles because of that fuel. Even though many people have subscribed to the philosophy of "If it feels good, do it," I doubt if many of them are going to pour gasoline onto the floors of their home and light it. They realize it will burn part or all of the house and maybe even them. And yet, people do that with their own freedom. They don't want limits.

Yet, gasoline should be limited to an internal combustion engine. If it's thrown on the floor of your house and lit, it won't serve its intended purpose.

So our personal freedoms must be limited to that which is beneficial and helpful and not given over to just anything. That's why crime is rampant in our nation; multiplied thousands of people believe freedom means freedom to steal, cheat, embezzle, lie, rape, commit mayhem, and do whatever they please. They have thrown caution to the winds, and we are reaping the whirlwind. Unhappiness and destruction lie in the wake of those who have thrown away all restraints.

Understand Yourself

A second clue is to understand yourself. Gautama Buddha taught that the path to happiness is true insight. Many people have false insights about themselves. These misconceptions are also bluesprints. They make comments like, "Things never turn out right for me. Well, I can't do anything right. Nobody likes me. My life is worthless." Even for the most pathetic, those are not true insights. Unless such false, angst-producing thoughts are changed, the pursuit of happiness will always be a slippery treadmill. It'll trip you up. In order to be happy, we must understand ourselves. Bluesprints snatch away a realistic perception of yourself.

Energize Yourself

Buddha's third central factor in developing happiness is using energy to produce healthy, uplifting thoughts. Early on I established that positive thinking is hard work because our natural inclination is toward the blues. Since overcoming the prints that are blue calls for energy, we must summon intense emotional and mental strength. Energy emanates from desire and determination.

Creative people who earn their living from writing, painting, sculpting, and the like have mentioned to me, "There are times I simply must force my creativity, or I would never do anything." That's true for custodians, bricklayers, carpenters, secretaries, salespersons—all of us. If we merely sit and wait for the impulse to strike us, it may never happen. From deep within we must determine, "I'm gonna do it. I may not want to work today, but I will. I may not want to write on my manuscript. I may not want to lay a brick, write

a letter, or paint a stroke—either on canvas or on a wall, but I must."
Then do it.

Once one truly recognizes the value of positive thinking, of avoiding blueprints, and of making other people happy, one will bend every effort to redirect and control his emotions and thinking. Without emotion-empowered energy, a person will, like a chameleon, conform to his negative environment. Which path do you follow? Do you "change colors," conforming to the mediocre, negative patterns around you, or do you have the energy to resist the bluesprints that cause you to be ineffective and unproductive?

Firm Up Yourself

A fourth clue is to be firm in pursuing good thoughts. There are literally hundreds of ads in the media about firming up one's body, even a videotape mainly for women entitled "Buns of Steel." It's a shame that many people spend countless hours firming up every part of their bodies but practically no time developing their flabby, out-of-shape minds. Firming up the mind means that you stick to a consistent, daily program of paring away those bluesprints and creating a mental and emotional atmosphere for solid thinking. It might even help to write it down and display it: "Positive thinking without positive behavior leads to delusion."

Speak for Yourself

A fifth pivotal factor leading to happiness is "good talking." Gautama referred to "proper discourse" as leading to happiness. His was an old-fashioned expression meaning "good words." Words spoken or thought can either raise a person to ecstasy or crush him to ashes. So, think those good words and repulse the bad ones. Try speaking the good, or don't speak at all. If you are in management and you have to discipline an employee, why not start with complimenting him? Surely he has at least one commendable quality, so praise him for it. If he doesn't why did your company hire him in the first place?

Happy People Fix the Problem—Not the Blame

It is my fond hope you have never labored for a boss who "managed by walking around" with a wrong motive, constantly trying to fix blame even before there was a problem. That sort of paranoid personality speaks loudly about the kind of person he is: insecure, unstable, and unable to trust others.

Here's another characteristic of happy people—happy people fix the problem and not the blame. First, let's touch on problems.

From Cheese to Mountains

A young grocery clerk once became tired of slicing pieces of cheese for every customer off of the same unsanitary wheel-like saw. Then J. L. Kraft, the founder of the Kraft Foods empire, fixed the problem and invented pre-packaged cheese. The Kraft name is now a household word. He could have camped on the blame—the old-fashioned wheel; instead he solved the problem.

A pineapple grower in Hawaii became exasperated with seeing pineapples rotting because people couldn't eat all he could grow fast enough. There was his problem, but Mr. Dole didn't blame a soul. Instead, he fixed the problem and began selling canned pineapple. Another household word.

A printing salesman once grew weary of eating in poor restaurants. So Duncan Hines fixed the problem and not the blame. He started his own restaurant and then later traveled all over the world, eating at restaurants and then rating them. Back then the highest commendation an eating place could receive was "Recommended by Duncan Hines." Then his own line of foods followed, including his cake mixes.

Years ago a young father became upset with having to mash up peas for his baby. It wasn't the biggest deal in the world. Gerber simply didn't like the situation, so he fixed the problem by inventing modern baby food. The face of the "Gerber baby" is recognized around the world.

I have already touched on this earlier, but happy people realize that problems are necessary for progress. They understand the value of their problems and the necessity to work on them. Sir Edmund Hillary and his Sherpa guide Tensing Norgay were the first people known to climb Mount Everest, the highest mountain on earth. Everest was a seemingly insurmountable problem. The New Zealander and the Sherpa studied the climb from every possible angle and standpoint and then climbed it.

After the fact Hillary declared, "I conquered Mount Everest." He had seen Everest as an obstacle, keeping him away from his ultimate goal. But Tensing Norgay, far more in touch with nature, explained, "The mountain and I together scaled the heights." Far more than Hillary, the Sherpa viewed the problem as an opportunity.

All According to Your Viewpoint

If you see your situations as problems, then that's what they're going to be. If you can learn to become positive, and view situations as opportunities, then they will appear vastly different to you. Then you'll be empowered to fix the problem and not the blame.

If I have the belief that I can do it I shall surely acquire the capacity to do it even if I may not have it at the beginning.

–Mahatma Gandhi

Things do not get better by being left alone.

— Winston Churchill

If you only knock long enough and loud enough at the gate, you are sure to wake somebody.

— Henry Wadsworth Longfellow

14

EIGHT PRACTICAL STEPS TO PROBLEM-SOLVING

THERE ARE ABOUT AS MANY ways and means of dealing with problems as there are people. Of course, the House of Representatives in Washington has its own Ways and Means Committee, but who knows if it's solving any problems? Here are eight Mindrobics strategies of fixing problems.

1. *Gather data.* It all depends on how pressing and urgent the problem is, whether it is one that calls for immediate handling or another that requires solving over the long haul. Regardless, if you have a problem, research it and discover all you can about it. Also talk with those who have gone through a similar problem. It's infinitely better to jump into a problem with your eyes wide open than to grapple with totally unknown, unanticipated qualities and quantities. Happy people are informed people.

2. *Define your problem(s) before you tackle it(them).* Try to establish exactly what the problem is. It's not enough to run around wringing your hands and lamenting, "We've got a problem. We've

got a problem." What precisely is the problem? The entire history of the world might have been different if movers and shakers had adequately identified their problems, and we might have undergone far fewer wars and international disasters.

3. *Determine the hoped-for outcome.* What do you want to accomplish? If you don't have the foggiest notion what you're after, you certainly won't know how to solve a problem. Does that make sense?

4. *Search for possible solutions.* Once people have defined what they want to accomplish with their problem, they need to begin looking for possible approaches and solutions that will lead to a resolution of the problem. Sometimes that will be easy, and an answer may be worked out within a matter of minutes. I wish that were always the case, but it unfortunately is not—it may require an extended period, depending on the problem. Those involved in the problem-solving must focus on those possible solutions.

5. *Choose what you feel is the best solution.* Many problems do not have a fantastic, magnificent, fantabulous solution, to use exaggerated superlatives. The solution may seem pitiful, but it may be the best you have, so a piece of solution is better than no solution at all. Happy, positive people, though, opt for the best solution available and run with it. If it's found faulty, and they can later think of better adaptations, they act upon those.

6. *Implement your strategy.* Do it. Take action. On nearly every page of this book, we have touched on the power of action. Positive people, once they choose the best solution, move to put it into action. Quite frankly too many organizations, government agencies, and businesses allegedly hammer out solutions that then lie dormant in multipage documents that keep transcriptionists, typesetters, and printers busy—but, alas, the solutions are never activated.

7. *Evaluate the outcomes.* Positive people, in problem solving, are not content to lean back smugly, bragging, "Hey, aren't we great problem-solvers? Aren't these recommendations terrific?" They continue to evaluate the outcomes of their suggestions, always testing them with the question, "Did we attain the sought-after results?" If they didn't ...

8. *Repeat the entire process, if necessary.* History is resplendent with examples of this—Henry Ford, for instance. He went through two bankruptcies but finally succeeded on his third attempt. Thomas

Alva Edison, considered by many the most influential inventor of all time, tried ninety-six elements for his electric light bulb before he happened on tungsten. It worked! But he at first failed ninety-six times. How many of us would do that?

Differences of opinion should never mean hostility.
— Mahatma Gandhi

Rare is the person who can weigh the faults of others without putting his thumb on the scales.
— Byron J. Longenfeld

If you want to travel far and fast, travel light. Take off your envies, jealousies, unforgiveness, selfishness, and fears.

— Glen Clark

15

DON'T PLAY THE BLAME GAME

HAPPY PEOPLE EXAMINE how to solve their problems and not to blame "the fickle finger of fate" or circumstances or adversities or others. Negative people are controlled by fixing blame. "Who's to blame for this fix I'm in? Who's plotting against me?"

Of course, blame began a long time ago. Zig Ziglar has commented, "Blame goes all the way back to the Garden of Eden. Adam blamed Eve, and Eve turned around and blamed the serpent, and the poor serpent didn't have a leg to stand on!" And it is true — blame makes you lame.

An unknown writer defined blame like this: "If you lower your bucket into life's well, lengthen your rope. Don't kick the bucket." Those are the two behaviors. Unhappy people "kick the bucket." Unhappy folks blame, accuse, and become all bent out of shape. Happy people, when they try a venture and their bucket comes up empty, lengthen their rope.

What's Bad About Blame

You might remark, "Wait a minute, Steve. Shouldn't somebody be blamed if things don't go the way we want them to?" Let me answer by explaining reasons why blame is not a worthy approach to life.

Reason number one is: blame makes a person a victim. For instance, if I am the way I am because my wife is treating me in a certain manner, then I have become a victim. There's nothing I can do about it if she's responsible and to blame. She's at fault. If I'm the way I am because my dad whipped me too much when I was a child, then I'm stuck. If my business is on the rocks and it is because of the economy or because of the current president, then I'm not at fault. Hey, I can't do anything about it. Hey, I'm a victim. I'm in the pits because of the economy or whatever. Some people blame recession; others inflation.

Yet, positive people guard against that fix-the-blame attitude. Negative blaming does nothing but immobilize the finger-pointer and keeps him from doing better about his situation. When blamers accuse others, they have become the "poor-little-me" victims. When you have a problem, of course you can exercise several options, but blaming someone is admitting defeat and that a situation is completely beyond your control, so there's nothing you can do.

Positive people surmount that. If I accept at least part of the responsibility for being the way I am—regardless of my parents, where I grew up, my peer group, my teachers, my coaches, etc.—I am no longer a victim. So, I can change matters. If I helped make me the way I am, then all of a sudden, I have bright rays of hope because I'm not stuck. Positive people choose that option. If his business isn't doing well, a positive person will confess, "I am at least partly responsible." Then all of a sudden I am empowered to do what I can and to take action.

Tell me. Have you ever met a happy victim? If you are a self-produced victim, you are not happy. Decide to accept responsibility. Quit blaming everybody but yourself. Maybe you have heard of singer-song writer-author Jimmy Buffett, who is still best known for his number-one hit "Margaritaville." He's "wastin' away again in Margaritaville, searchin' for my long-lost jigger of salt. Some people claim that there's a woman to blame ..." In the song his life is going down the tubes because of a woman—but finally it closes out with the candid confession: "Some people claim that there's a woman to blame, but I know it's my own fault."

Reason number two is that blame, along with hatred and resentment, is a potent negative emotion that literally nips happiness in the bud. Blame is invariably accompanied by resentment and ultimately intense dislike or hatred.

Hate is how we punish ourselves for the negative actions of others. Harry Emerson Fosdick, a famous preacher of an earlier generation, noted, "Hating people is like burning down your own house to get rid of a rat!" There is nothing to commend bitterness or hatred. One who hates may briefly feel a twisted sense of satisfaction, but the end result is lasting damage to himself. There is an ancient story that Caesar's troops were angry with the gods because the battle was not tilting in Rome's favor. They decided to punish the gods and goddesses by firing volleys of arrows toward the heavens. The arrows, of course, returned to earth, piercing many of the soldiers in the head and killing them. That is precisely what negative emotions will do to you.

On a day-to-day basis, this happens to you. Your life is jeopardized by careless drivers who tailgate you, sideswipe you, run traffic lights and stop signs, and drive with reckless abandon. Maybe one of those drivers has almost slammed into you. At first you were scared and breathed a sigh of relief, but then your emotions switched to irritation and maybe even livid rage. In such a predicament, unless you're careful you'll be tempted to yell at them or maybe even give them a certain "salute" with your middle finger. Meanwhile, though, that irresponsible driver has driven along and is probably not even aware of your existence. You are allowing that episode to dredge up dark feelings, and that driving culprit is hardly aware of you at all.

That triad of anger, bitterness, and blame has done nothing positive for you. Now Friedrich Nietzsche is not known for being the most delightful philosopher in the world, but this quotation does bear repeating: "Nothing on earth consumes a man more completely than the passion of resentment." From a different side of the spectrum, Will Rogers quipped, "People who fly into a rage almost always make a bad landing." But how can we possibly avoid blaming people and circumstances?

How Can We Avoid Blaming People and Circumstances?

One way is never to be hurt—but that's impossible, because everyone alive has been hurt by someone or something. Yes, you've been mistreated. Double affirmative, this is an unfair world. Certain people, though, seem to think that truly happy people are never mistreated. Nothing could be farther from the facts. Sometimes happy people have been mistreated even more than "the miserables." What's the difference? Happy people have backed away from assessing blame.

Here's another elementary method of avoiding blame: Perspective. It means to observe the entire situation in the proper light. Suppose you are helping a blind person across the street, and suddenly a bus roars by, missing you both by a foot or two. Suppose then that the blind man panics and starts swinging his cane, hitting your arm several times. It hurts like crazy, too.

Right off, you try to calm him down and stop his swinging of the cane. You protect yourself and try to keep him from hitting you in the head, but you don't feel bitter toward him. Surely, for the rest of your life, you wouldn't cop out with, "Well, twenty years ago this blind man did this, and that's why I'm not doing any better than I am."

You wouldn't do that. But why not? Because you would have the right slant on the situation. You would analyze what is happening: "The fellow is blind. He's hitting me, but it's accidental, and he's not really out to hurt me. He's reacting this way because of his own lack of vision, not because of me."

By reasoning with yourself through self-talk, you would not feel negative emotions toward the blind man. That example applies to what?

... to most anything anybody anytime anywhere does to you!

Don't Put the Blame on Mame

Maybe I'm off base, but I fully believe that when most people do others wrong, it's because of their own blindness, insecurity, and emotional pain. This or that has spooked them, and they are often hitting you with their cane. Yet, not being able to grasp that, we often respond with bitterness and blaming.

Have you ever heard a husband or a wife complain about a spouse, "Well, twenty years ago he (she) did blah, blah, blah, blah?" What a crying shame to carry that kind of negative marital baggage all those years! Have you ever stopped to think that he (she) did blah, blah, blah because of their own pain and insecurities? Maybe that "beloved other" was not really after you but merely reacting from foggy vision or no vision at all.

Learning from Door-to-Door Sales

This technique was imbedded into my brain years ago when I sold books from door to door for the Southwestern Company of Nashville. The first time a person slammed their door is my face, I was livid with rage. "That dirty jerk," I muttered under my breath. "How could he do that to me, a struggling book salesman trying to work his way through college?"

Work-wise, times are vastly different today. Back then the majority of wives worked at home instead of on the outside, so most of the people who hurt my feelings were women. But then I'd think it through: She's in there with kids—maybe sick ones, yelling ones, crying ones, squirming ones. She may not have a fan or air-conditioner. Maybe the water was boiling. Who knows what's going on behind that door, regardless of its color? "Green door, what's that secret you're keeping?" There's no telling what made her react as she did.

When I refocused and reframed the situation from that standpoint, helping me to recognize that the door-slammers were not necessarily after me, how could I harbor ill feelings toward them? They no doubt had problems, upsets, blind spots. Maybe their husbands were cheating on them while they were stuck at home with screaming, unruly kids—maybe even at that moment hubby was out to lunch with a girl friend. Or their husband was being laid off from his job. Thousands of possibilities existed, so why did I have to take that as being personal against me?

I could even feel kindness and mercy for those people. You see, faults are like headlights. Other people's faults only seem to be more glaring than our own. We have to keep a balance. Even though we want to have a healthy self-image and to project self-esteem, we must not have a distorted self-image that causes us to overlook a still-glaring reality: we all have faults.

113

One perspective that helps us to avoid blaming others is: realize that wrong is often a two-way street. No doubt, unless you are a rare duck, you have done somebody wrong somewhere along the line. Perhaps you were not even aware of it. Notice how it balances out? We're all in this together as fellow members of the human race.

Wayne Dyer wisely wrote, "Your hurts come, not from what others do to you, but from what you choose to do with their actions." It's not what they've done. It's how you've viewed it. Epictetus opined, "It is not he who gives abuse that affronts, but it's the view we take of it as insulting." When someone provokes you, it is your own opinion that magnifies the provocation. It's how you look at it—what you're telling yourself, your perspective.

Tips on Dealing with the Blame Game

Another way to deal with your feelings is to concede goodwill. Become an inverse paranoid. I love that statement. I'm kind of an inverse paranoid. I think everybody's out to ... not get me . . . but help me. Of course, I may be kidding myself—you may all be out to get me—but it surely makes me feel better to give everybody the benefit of the doubt and to believe that everybody's out to *help* me.

Yes, I realize in the real world there are people out to hurt you, but in most cases those people have a bundle of insecurities, and they're like the blind man or the door-slammer. Really believe most people are out to help, not hinder you.

The Free Flight of Forgiveness

Another means of avoiding the blame game is to forgive. Now you are familiar with that word; because of how it's often used you may feel I am plunging into religion here, but forgiveness is not simply a religious term. It's patently a fact of life, a powerful tool for not being eaten up with blame and resentment. Of course, people remark, "I can forgive, but I can't forget." Well, there's a difference between forgiving and forgetting. Forgetting, of course, means that you no longer remember the wrong that was done.

Earlier in this book, I mentioned the guy who promised me a windfall if I would invest $4,000 of my hard-earned money in fire alarms. I sold none. That fire-alarm salesman assured me I'd make $30,000 part-time the first year. I remember the deal and the circumstances, or I couldn't write about it here. I recall all the details, and yet I no longer feel negative emotions toward the salesman, because I forgave him.

To forgive means to give up any claims to feel negatively about the act, deed, or event that was "done" to you. It's basically agreeing with your heart of hearts, "OK, I release it. I let it go." When you've forgiven, you may occasionally think about the wrong that was done, but you won't feel resentment or bitterness. Also, if you have genuinely forgiven, you will not intentionally dredge up the wrong done to you and use it as a truncheon against your emotions or the feelings of others involved.

Often I have heard people adamantly snarl, "I can never forgive what he's done." "She's dead meat as far as I'm concerned." "No way, forgiveness is out of the question!" Really, how does one forgive?

1. *Just decide you want to forgive.* If you're blaming someone, you're putting yourself in the role of a victim, and you're going to be miserable. I repeat it: happy people don't waste their lives blaming other people. So you must reach the crossroads where you decide, "I want to forgive. I don't know if I can or not, but I don't like having these beastly feelings toward people."

2. *So once you decide, the second step is to declare out loud, "I completely forgive so and so for such and such."* "I totally forgive the person who sold me those fire alarms and took $4,000 of my money."

Merely by making the statement of forgiveness—the intent of forgiveness—you will experience an incredible release inside. It will break your chains of emotional bondage. Before your willingness to forgive, your entire life has been ominously darkened by bitterness, anger, resentment, hatred, and innumerable ghouls that live in your subconscious. Ah, the free flight of forgiveness! You can let go of blame if you honestly want to release it. Sure, you can hold onto it if you want to, but it will not only "eat your lunch," it will eat your life. Happy people have learned to let go. I have never known a truly happy person who was unforgiving.

3. *The next step is to make the conscious declaration, "I refuse to think accusing thoughts or have bad feelings toward the person I have forgiven."* Now and then you will have to debate with yourself when those blueprints of unforgiveness crawl into the corners of your mind. Kill that impulse as you would a black widow or brown recluse

spider or a rattlesnake. Refuse to dwell on the wrong and the person who committed it. After all, you have forgiven him. You have released that person—and thus have released yourself to have a victorious life. You have given up all rights to nurse negative thoughts or emotions about him and what he did.

Forgiveness flies in the face of "human nature." It doesn't come naturally; there is a touch of the Divine in it. As you continue to forgive, even though tempted to renege, you will experience a "rush" of freedom and liberty of conscience, emotions, heart, mind, and will.

You are unusual if several people have not wronged you over a period of time. I can think of several who have grieved me severely, and I could have dug my own snake pits of resentment through the years. Instead, I have forgiven them.

Forgive Yourself!

How strange it is that many of us seem capable of forgiving others but cannot seem to forgive ourselves! Yes, we have responsibility for ourselves. Sure, we will screw up all too often, but we do not have to beat ourselves up over it. As a human being, you've made your share of mistakes. You may ask, "How does he know that about me?" No sweat. Like it or not we're related to the earthly family, and we've all messed up.

In certain countries there are religious zealots who, at certain holy seasons of the year, torture themselves, especially by walking through the streets beating themselves with chains, whips, and barbed wire. They are referred to as flagellantes. They no doubt are consecrated but sadly mistaken, for they are allegedly trying to gain merit and to atone for their sins. Now, before we start pointing the finger at them, what about us who are doing exactly the same to ourselves, only whipping ourselves emotionally, mentally, physically, and spiritually by putting ourselves down with negative, unproductive practices and mind-sets?

Certainly, forgive others ... but also forgive yourself. Go through the same process you did in forgiving others. Say out loud, "I completely forgive myself for the stupidity that I showed when I bought those fire alarms." Then, refuse to accuse yourself. You have dealt with it. You probably can't forget it; you will also recall that you did it, but when you remember, you won't wallow in adverse emotions. You won't be devoured by it.

Stop "Shoulding" Yourself!

Another serious situation we create for ourselves is: we should ourselves. Do you ever should on yourself? We often assume that we should measure up to other people's standards, whether parents, a business associate, a sports figure, or a minister, priest, or rabbi. (Many of the unhappiest people I have encountered were those who followed a certain profession, not because they really wanted to, but because mother or dad or another "role model" would have been disappointed if they had not. They were taught they "should" enter the ministry, "should" become an M.D., "should" become a nun.)

Here I go again: many sad folks feel that "should" simply happens, that putting should on themselves is normal and expected, but should is what people do to themselves.

How many times have you heard, "I should have done this. I should do that"? There is another unfruitful, unproductive activity, spending precious energy and time "shoulding" over the past. "I should have done that. I should do this tomorrow." They should all over themselves. Well, what good is a self-inflicted should? What beneficial purpose does it serve?

Reasons for Bypassing "Should"

Why, surely we should appreciate should! Oh, really? OK, if you should, why haven't you? If you should have, why didn't you? If you should tomorrow, why don't you? What's negative and uncreative about should?

1. Should makes you feel guilty all the time.

2. It makes you feel shame.

3. It makes you feel unhappy.

4. It makes you feel stress when you're frequently saying, "I should do this. I should have done that. I should do this or that later. I need to be doing that."

5. It makes you feel you are under domination of forces outside of yourself, and there's nothing you can do about it.

6. It makes you feel as if you are a victim, that you have no right to your own decisions, what you want to do, or where you want to go.

7. It also makes you feel like you do not and cannot measure up.

8. It makes you feel inferior.

117

Is that what you want? Personally, I have never enjoyed shame or undue stress or being a victim or victimizing myself or feelings of inferiority. Projecting should onto the past by alibiing, "I should have," changes nothing. It is usually too late to amend yesterday. Instead of saying, "I should have," a positive person asserts, "Next time I will." He uses hopeful language. Anticipation and excitement are integral parts of such affirmations.

The same is true of laying should on the present or the future by saying, "I should do this." But positive people don't say, "I should do this." Instead, they just do it! They don't should themselves into it. Saying "I should," and doing nothing about it only produces unpleasant or painful emotions. If I tell myself, "I should," and I fail to follow through, it lowers my self-esteem and feelings of worth.

You see, if you feel you must speak about your intentions, say "I will," not "I should." "I will" means that you are acting of your own free will, and "should" means that you're being compelled. Should is a hard habit to break. I dare not tell you that you should break the should habit—because that would be doing the same thing—but I highly recommend it.

Positive, happy people live life virtually without the should syndrome. They've gone beyond it, beyond the blame, beyond the accusations of other people, beyond the accusations of themselves, and they're living life more as they desire, taking responsibility and fixing the problem, not the blame.

Slap Those Killer Bees

Happy people do not become involved with what I call "killer bees." Believe me, they are swarming to sting you. Beware, those pesky rascals may be buzzing inside your head as you read this.

Some killer bees: Killer Bee Negative. The classic sourpuss pessimist has been stung by this killer bee. Most everybody in our society has been stung a little bit by the killer bee negative. When it stings you, you'll start to concentrate on all the bad stuff in your life, and if you're not careful, you'll soon forget about all the goodies.

Then you'll start the blame game all over again, pointing fingers at others instead of shouldering responsibility. How to protect yourself from killer bee negative? Slap that critter down before it stings you. But if it's already stung you, and you're sort of negative, a shot of appreciation would help. If you will gratefully think about or remember something good in your life, killer bee negative will fly away to his horrid hive.

Another killer bee is Killer Bee Bitter. We have looked at him all through this section on blaming. This noxious insect penetrates deeply and causes excruciating pain. The wound, however, heals nicely unless you pick at it. In that case, it can turn into a festering inner sore. The only prescription for freedom from its pain is to completely forgive. Many people needlessly suffer a lifetime from the bite of this bitter bee, because they're too proud to dispense with the offense and to submerge it into forgiveness.

In their minds, the agony of bitterness somehow evens the score. I hope you've seen from the positive characteristics that happy people fix the problem and not the blame and that bitterness never makes it right.

It is not how much we have but how much we enjoy that makes happiness.
— Charles Haddon Spurgeon

It came to me that having life itself, life being such a miraculous achievement, is like winning the grand prize. What we do after that—what we do with our lives—is the frosting on the cake.
— Earl Nightingale

Many people need more hope than help. Keep hope alive.
— Jesse Jackson

16

HAPPY PEOPLE ENUMERATE THEIR NON-FINANCIAL ASSETS

Y OU MIGHT REMARK, "Hey, he's finally come to my favorite subject—money, moolah, finances, bread, the folding green, dollars!" Not really.

Once I counted my financial assets. They appeared rather negative. Of course, it is not a snap to be positive about financial negatives. Earlier in this book I pointed out a cardinal reality: people who depend on financial success alone in order to obtain happiness . . . will never be truly happy. One cannot buy genuine happiness, love, satisfaction, dignity, and self-esteem.

Happy people enumerate—add up—their non-financial assets in addition to their financial ones.

It seems that regardless of monetary income, most everyone has difficulties at one time or another. If a person is making a considerable amount, he still seems to spend most of it, and he yearns for more to support his life-style. If one is making a moderate living or less, he tries to live within his means, on the edge, or beyond them.

Call me blessed or fortunate, but I've never had a deficit in my non-financial assets. Maybe there are times when I thought I did—when I was feeling down and discouraged, when I was toying with dragging out my bluesprints.

Count Your Blessings, Not Your Banes

What about you? Many people were born with handicaps. Are you grateful for your faculties if you have them—hearing, seeing, touching, tasting, feeling? People have actually asked questions like, "Would you take a million dollars for one of your five senses?" Of course not, yet we read that in certain poverty-ridden areas of the world people are selling their internal organs or other body parts for paltry sums.

Several years ago, I spent three months teaching and speaking throughout India. By and large, India is a destitute nation of over 900,000,000. It is estimated 200,000,000 live in the streets. In the U.S. the homeless amount to no more than three million. That is deplorable but nothing to compare with Third Word countries. In most Third World countries children are often gladly sold for a pittance.

Here in the U.S.A. a couple of years ago, I spent a night with six homeless men who were housed and fed by a ministry called Room in the Inn. I talked at length with them and found they were in fairly good shape. They had food, clothing, a reasonably comfortable place to stay, and, believe it or not, they were better off than 80 percent of India's population. No wonder, in the words of Neil Diamond's song, "They're Coming to America." In fact, they're doing that to the extent that Congress is tightening its cap on immigration.

It Can Be a Wonderful Life

Perhaps many moderns think the movie "It's a Wonderful Life" is corny because it is rather melodramatic and emphasizes those so-called "old-time values." Actually, there is nothing old-time about them because they still reap benefits today. No doubt you have seen that movie with Jimmy Stewart and Donna Reed at least once, if not dozens of times.

You remember that in the story Jimmy Stewart, as George Bailey, followed in his honest father's footsteps and tried to make housing affordable for hard-working citizens during and at the end of World War II. Lionel Barrymore, a crooked business boss in the town and the "villain," tried to put George out of business. Through chicanery Barrymore forced the bank to the point of foreclosing on all the mortgages of Bailey's home buyers. A heavy snow was falling as George Bailey, crushed and humiliated, staggered to a bridge on the edge of town, ready to jump into icy river waters and drown himself.

Remember? But an old man, actually an angel on assignment (played by Henry Travers), was screaming "Help!" from the raging waters. George jumped in and rescued the "angel unawares."

George commiserated to the angel, "I wish I had never been born," so the angel granted his wish. The angel appeared here and there as George returned to the once kindly, genteel town, now one of ill will, debauchery, and disdain for humanity. He went to a cemetery and saw his brother's grave, but George protested, "But I saved my brother's life when he was a kid." The angel replied, "Oh, but you've never been born. There was no one there to save your brother's life."

In one incident after another, George was shown that his life had made a vast difference in the lives of the town and its people. George Bailey was able to enumerate his non-financial assets. By the time he passed through all those life-without-George-Bailey experiences, he begged the angel to recreate his life as it was, even with all its problems, because now there was a sense that he had made a difference and that all was not lost. You may recall that the movie ended happily. Donations from friends all over flooded in to cover the mortgage payments that were due the bank the following morning!

Appreciate the Simple Things

Happy, positive people may not possess scads of money and fame. that many are pursuing to give them happiness or status. Happy people — rich, in-between, or poor financially — have learned to appreciate the simple things.

It would pay all of us to learn the lyrics of "The Best Things in Life Are Free." The song, often sung in the Great Depression, enumerates the moon, the stars, and the flowers, and it closes, "And love can come to anyone. The best things in life are free."

To find happiness avail yourself of nature's inspiration. Just open your eyes and look around at the trees, the mountains, the plants, the birds, the animals, bodies of water from a creek to an ocean, the moon, the stars, the clouds, the "Starry, starry night," about which Don MacLean sang in "Vincent." Emerson had a phrase for it: "The sky is the daily bread of the eyes." Here's an adage and a song, "Stop and Smell the Roses."

Alfred Kimbourg expressed this sentiment with ... "The sky is that beautiful old parchment in which the sun and the moon keep their diary." John Ruskin, rare author and artist, noted: "Nature is painting for us, day after day, pictures of infinite beauty, if we only had eyes to see them." Then Luther Burbank, the remarkable botanist, said, "Flowers are sunshine, food, and medicine to the soul."

Why is it people think they have to buy happiness? Happiness is right at your fingertips. You are cheating yourself if you fail to "cash in" on your non-financial assets. Not long ago I viewed a group of world-famous paintings known as "Masterworks," owned by Bridgestone Museum of Art in Tokyo. Those masterpieces are valued into the mega-millions of dollars.

But you can walk outside on a starry night and behold a breathtaking expanse of grandeur far more precious than all of those paintings put together. Now, I hope you are financially successful. But you can never place an order for happiness because it is not for sale. What counts is appreciation and enumerating your assets.

Examples of Enumerators

Franklin Delano Roosevelt, U.S. president from 1933 until his death in 1945, was most of his adult life paralyzed by polio from his waist down. Many historians place him in a league with Washington, Jefferson, Lincoln, and Wilson. Roosevelt led his nation through two of its most perilous periods, the Great Depression and World War II.

He remarked on one occasion, "Once I spent two years lying in bed trying to move my big toe. That was the hardest job I ever had to do. After that, anything else seems easy!" Even though FDR was wealthy, intelligent, and revered around the world, he understood how to enumerate his non-financial assets. He was positive; in spite of severe handicaps he decisively guided the most powerful nation in the world. He gloried in being able to move his big toe. He was able to accentuate the "little things."

Earlier on I referred to Helen Keller, who was stricken blind, deaf, and mute at age two. Yet, she became one of the most erudite authors and personalities of her day. Annie Sullivan was her devoted tutor who helped Helen to learn special communication skills. The play and movie "The Miracle Worker" related the stirring story of Annie Sullivan and Helen Keller's relationship.

At the end of Keller's life, she summed it up, "I have found life so beautiful." That is incredible. How could she possibly make that statement? Far too many folks who seem to "have everything going for them" gripe all the time and are never satisfied. The difference? She learned to count her blessings, not her banes. She was adding up her positive ledger, not moaning over her adversities but making merry over her assets.

To me this quotation from Keller ("Three Days to See," *Reader's Digest*, March 1933) reaches the pinnacle of inspiration:

> I, who am blind, can give one hint to those who see. Use your eyes as if tomorrow you'd be stricken blind. And the same method can be applied to the other senses. Hear the musical voices, the song of a bird, the mighty strains of an orchestra as if you would be stricken deaf tomorrow. Touch each object as if tomorrow your tactile sense would fail you. Smell the perfume of flowers. Taste with relish each morsel as if tomorrow you could never smell and taste again. Make the most of every sense. Glory in all the facets of pleasure and beauty which the world reveals to you through the several means of contact which nature provides. But of all the senses, I am sure sight must be most delightful.

Helen Keller enumerated her non-financial assets. She avoided self-pity. Rather than lamenting over her missing physical senses, she rejoiced over her spiritual senses, her anticipation not only of this life but the life that lay beyond. She was able to see the unseeable and hear the unhearable. She met presidents, kings, ambassadors, and other celebrities, but her persona was more radiant than them all. In fact, those who came in contact with her remarked that she was probably the most appreciative person they had ever known. Keller was happier than most seeing and hearing people, because she zestfully cherished what she did have.

South Vietnam — 29 May 1969 — Tommy Clark was hit by an artillery shell. It blew off both of his legs above the knee, and it tore off his right arm at the shoulder. Tommy spent twenty-one months in various hospitals, undergoing thirty operations. He was finally released almost two years later in March 1971.

Tommy admits he was able to keep a positive attitude those two years in the hospital because—and this is a quote—"I always was around people who were worse off than I was. I felt lucky I had what I had left. God left me with a good mind, a gift of gab, and a strong heart, and I try to make the best of these each day."

Although confined to a wheelchair, Tommy has traveled to all fifty states as a speaker. He has coordinated political campaigns for local, state, and national candidates, and he has served as a staff assistant to the director of the Atlanta VA for over ten years.

In 1989 Tommy was elected the Outstanding Disabled Veteran of the Year. Both legs and one arm torn off, in horrible shape, and yet he was able to remain positive. Yep, he enumerated his non-financial assets. Throughout his ordeal and today, he recognizes it could have been worse!

It's Crucial: Pay Attention to What You Have

Stick this on your bulletin board. What you pay attention to grows. Positive people have learned (and it's not an easy lesson) to pay attention to what they have rather than what they lack. Helen Keller paid attention to her keen mind and valiant spirit, not her blindness and deafness. Wake up! Play up your good points. Ignore your bad. Count your non-financial assets. I guarantee you that your life will be better.

Richard DeVoss, a co-founder of the Amway Corporation, helps me underline the above principle: "I believe in an upward look. Given the option to read life however I choose, I believe in underlining the positive passages with a bright-red pencil, and skipping over the negative ones with barely a glance."

Just Do It!

Accentuate the positives in your life.

Underline them.

Pay attention to them.

Conversely, what does that involve? Push the negatives aside.

Thomas Dryer advised:

> When you talk about your troubles, your ailments, your diseases, your hurts, you give longer life to what makes you unhappy. Talking about your grievances merely adds to those grievances. Give recognition only to what you desire. Think and talk only about the good things that add to your enjoyment of your work and life. If you don't talk about your grievances, you'll be delighted to find them disappearing quickly.

That technique actually works ... but you'll never know if you don't put it into practice. I repeat this only because it is essential: all of us have enough bad, negative experiences to immobilize us if we let them. We don't have everything we want; if we did we wouldn't recognize that we did, and we'd still be dissatisfied. We could concentrate on what's wrong in our lives and make ourselves emotionally and mentally sick, or we could emulate the people in this chapter—Helen Keller, Franklin Delano Roosevelt, Tommy Clark, and even fictional George Bailey. Rather than grousing we could glory in the good.

Remember when the angel allowed George Bailey back into real life. George sprinted through the snowy streets, cheering and yelling, happy that he had been born, even though he had to encounter problems that previously had driven him to the brink of suicide.

What If ... ?

At this moment maybe you feel you have been given a bum deal or dealt a bad hand. Yet, suppose for a moment that you lost everything you had like Job of the Bible did — your family, your possessions, your money, your house, everything. And suppose you were flat on your back in the hospital and you had nothing. But also suppose "The Good Fairy" or an angel entered your room and announced, "Even though you've lost all these things, I am giving them all back to you."

Stop and imagine how grateful you would feel just to get back what you lost and don't have. Now this technique is effective not only for people who are in less than the best shape physically. I never cease being amazed that people who are physically disabled seem to

127

overcome their handicaps by being positive. Yet, many people who are "in the pink" of health and "have it made" don't enjoy life until they have the jolt of a trauma to snap them out of their blase attitude about what constitutes bona fide happiness.

Unfortunately, I've found that's the case. It often seems that those who seem to have everything going their way, just don't appreciate what they have. The technique of this chapter will work for you, me, everyone, regardless of their financial, health, or social situation.

Talk It Up

The NCAA a few seasons ago imposed a new rule on college football teams. After scoring, a team is now not supposed to celebrate. Perhaps they used to carry it too far when twenty-five or thirty players would scurry to the end zone doing "high-fives," dancing like Tina Turner, and then falling on top of the guy who scored the touchdown or kicked the field goal.

Regardless, a lackluster team without enthusiasm is usually in the losing column. The winningest coaches in football history like Knute Rockne, Amos Alonzo Stagg, Bear Bryant, Joe Paterno, Lou Holtz, Vince Lombardi, Bud Wilkinson, and Frank Broyles encouraged their players to emphasize what they could do well and right.

Coaches have found that pep talks before games and at halftime are usually necessary. However, many of the most successful coaches ask the players to enumerate the team's good points. Yes, the team has watched game films and critiqued its performance the week before, pointing out missed tackles and blocks, botched assignments, and weaknesses right down to the slightest motion of a running back. But that's not enough. What's right about the team? Many a team has turned certain defeat into victory by emphasizing what they had, not what they lacked!

Jot 'em Down

If you're older than me you may remember the radio program "Lum 'n Abner." They were the proprietors of the "Jot-'em-Down" Store in rural Arkansas. I strongly advise you to start jotting down your non-financial assets. Devote one pad, notebook, or tablet to it—or maybe list those assets in your PC. Read the list in the morning and in the evening and continue that for three weeks, twenty-one days. The pluses will amaze you, and you will be happier for it.

Tips for Jotting 'em Down

1. *Make the list literal.* Write down or type the list. Keeping your list in your head is not enough.

2. *Make it exhaustive and expansive.* Write for as long as you can and keep adding to your asset list. If you can think of 500 assets, jot them down. Every day, when good things come about, add them to your ledger.

3. *Make it often-read.* Go over your asset list continually. Put it to practical use to lift up your spirit.

4. *Make it spoken.* Share it on occasion, but be sure you share it with friends. Also, don't brag. Simply express thanks. Thank others for the blessings they've given you. Thank God for His blessings. Speak about your blessings to other people, and you will find that you'll be happier than any drug can make you. Enumerating your non-financial assets is such a powerful tool.

Once upon a time I wrote a fiction piece about a woman who illustrates the contrast between people who use this positive enumeration technique and the negative pessimists who don't.

Mrs. Rubble and Emma Jean Goodthings

Mrs. Rubble was always unhappy. Nothing or no one could please her, and many people had tried. Once, after Mrs. Rubble was in the hospital, an elderly neighbor, Mary Blessing, brought over supper. But Mrs. Rubble wouldn't even eat that supper. No, she threw that meal into the trash, and she was growling, "The nerve of that woman, trying to tempt away my husband, Barney, with all this good food."

Well, once Barney won a new Cadillac in a local sweepstakes, and all Mrs. Rubble had to say about it was: "Barney ruined us. Now we've got to pay more taxes. We don't get nearly as much gas mileage, and our insurance has gone out of sight. And to top it off, now Barney has the big head. I'm afraid he's going to leave me now for sure."

Well, everybody in the community liked Barney and spoke well of him—everybody, that is, but you guessed it, his wife. She told a neighbor, "Everybody brags about Barney too much. So it's up to me to tell him his faults."

Across town, another woman named Emma Jean Goodthings lived. And Emma Jean Goodthings always thought the very best of everything and everybody. Once, when a grocery boy was carrying out her groceries, he stopped, looked her in the eye, and said, "Lady, you can carry your own blankety-blank groceries." He threw Emma Jean Goodthings's groceries down, got in his car, and drove away.

Several people heard Emma Jean Goodthings say, "That poor boy must have a terrible problem. I sure hope he gets to feeling better. I'd better go back in and get some more groceries." Guess what? She chuckled, "I'll probably get them for free this time. Oh, lucky me! I'll have some extra money this week."

Emma Jean Goodthings's attitude was indestructible. It seemed as if nothing could take away her smile. Then, guess again. Emma Jean Goodthings bumped into the Rubble's Cadillac. "Look what you did to my car. That dent looks like the Grand Canyon!" yelled Mrs. Rubble!

"Well, I'm sorry, Ma'am. Neither of us is hurt. It's a beautiful day. Besides, you don't have to worry about a thing. My insurance will be glad to fix that dent. I've got a piece of the rock." That's what Emma Jean said.

Then Mrs. Rubble said, "Maybe so, but I've got to fool with all those nasty mechanics. My husband will probably kill me, because of people like you who don't know how to drive. You keep running into innocent people like me," grumbled Mrs. Rubble.

"Well, Ma'am, all I can say is, if I hadn't bumped into your beautiful car, I would never have had the pleasure of meeting you. My name is Emma Jean Goodthings. What's yours?"

"Rubble, most people call me Mrs. Rubble."

"What a fine name," exclaimed Mrs. Emma Jean Goodthings. "I always liked Barney and Betty Rubble on the Flintstones when I was a child. They sure knew how to laugh their way through problems, didn't they?"

"I don't know. I never watch cartoons. They're too silly. I don't let my kids watch them either," groused Mrs. Rubble.

"Ah, but they can make you laugh. Would you like to join me for lunch, Mrs. Rubble?" asked Emma Jean Goodthings.

"Well, if you'll pay for it. You know, this old Cadillac is nothing but trouble. It cost me $7,000 in taxes, and it ..."

"Mrs. Rubble, what is your first name?" Emma Jean Goodthings asked.

"Joy—Joy Rubble is my real name, but no one ever calls me that."

"Well, come on, Joy Rubble. You and I are going to have a wonderful lunch and, I'm buying." Then a very odd thing happened. Mrs. Rubble smiled.

I like to end this story, "Come on, miserable. Start imaging good things, and you'll smile too." Those two women illustrate opposite attitudinal poles. Emma Jean Goodthings is always enumerating her non-financial assets, looking positively for the best in everything.

Mrs. Rubble, of course, is searching for and expecting the worst. She even telegraphs it. Are you imaging good things or are you miserable or are you struggling somewhere between the two?

Utilize the enumeration technique. Count those blessings. Make a list. Like Santa Claus "check it twice" and thrice and . . . make that list exhaustive, expansive, often-read, and spoken. Stick with it for three weeks, and the odds are you'll be happier than you've ever been.

Words are the most powerful drug used by mankind. Not only do words infect, egotize, narcotize, and paralyze, but they enter in and color the minutest calls of the brain.
— Rudyard Kipling

Words are magical in the way they affect the minds of those who use them.
— Aldous Huxley

The mere mental repetition of well-selected words and phrases will strengthen and stimulate your mind in a remarkable manner.
— Greenville Kleiser

17

A CLOSER LOOK AT MINDROBICS

HAPPY HUMAN BEINGS incorporate Mindrobics into their lives. "Mindrobics" is the term I have developed for the art of producing personal happiness. Dr. Kenneth Cooper, the founder of The Aerobics Center in Dallas, Texas, is the authority primarily responsible for popularizing the concept called "Aerobics." He, along with the late Jim Fixx, is known as a fellow who started America running. I appreciate Dr. Cooper. It is encouraging that today many people recognize the importance of regular physical exercise. Thank you, Dr. Cooper.

There's another form of exercise, though, that most folks seldom participate in or think about, and I would like to popularize that form of exercise. Mindrobics.

I define Mindrobics as the exercise of taking control of your mind and running it down a prescribed positive thought path on a regular basis. Mindrobics involves jogging your memory and re-experiencing your past victories and successes. It's the mental training process we've been discussing in this book.

As we have seen, most human pain and suffering are mental. Fear, worry, crime, drug and alcohol abuse, divorce, anxiety, bitterness, war, poverty, psychosomatic illnesses, and depression are all pushed along by faulty, wrong thinking and by mental surrender to a prevalently negative human environment.

Mindrobics, like Aerobics, enables a person to change his attitudes and behavior gradually. No one expects to change his body overnight, to train himself to become a physical champion in twenty-four hours. Yet, many of us expect our minds to respond that quickly. We are used to instant rice, potatoes, and coffee; we often dote on "fast food." When we embark on a new mental behavior, we have exaggerated expectations and want immediate success.

That's the equivalent of a paunchy, middle-aged man exercising three minutes to a vigorous exercise tape and then collapsing on the couch and concluding, "Whew, that Aerobics stuff just doesn't work. I'm through with it once and for all." Of course, he didn't give it a chance. The truth is: neither Mindrobics nor Aerobics will work for lazy folks.

Are You Willing?

If you're willing to make a long-term, committed effort, Mindrobics has proven techniques that will dramatically transform your life. Happy people use Mindrobics, whether or not they call it that.

Are you ready to stretch your mind? This is a Mindrobics session here. Maybe your mind's rather stiff and stunted, all boxed up with limiting beliefs and negative notions. This exercise will help pull you beyond your mental limits, and it's surprisingly invigorating. Ready? Mindrobics cannot help unless you do the exercises. Mindrobics, like Aerobics, is not a spectator sport. Just reading this is not sufficient. What do you have to lose? So, give this Mindrobics exercise a whirl with me. Here goes.

Locate a mirror and look into it, even if it scares you at first! After you read this, walk to the mirror and take a glance. Isn't that an attractive person there? If you're in your home, you can go to the bathroom and look in the mirror. Now you may not make it for the handsomest man or most beautiful woman in the world, but you're not that bad. In fact, there is a possibility you may be stunning.

Look yourself in the eyes and speak to yourself. No, this is not silly. Quote a song, maybe even, "Hey there, you with the stars in your eyes." Not bad for starters. Or even try the zany, "Lord, it's hard to be humble when you're perfect in every way!" Give yourself a sincere smile—no, not a smirk. Go ahead. Your face won't crack. Then stand there and gaze at yourself for a while. Do it. Don't be a stick in the mud.

I briefly touched on this exercise in an earlier chapter. Now we are moving into detail. As you look yourself in the eyes, say this phrase out loud, "I like myself." Pretend you're an actor. Say "I like myself" with enough conviction, sincerity, and enthusiasm to win an Academy Award. Do it. It won't hurt.

Did you do it? It feels pretty good, doesn't it? Maybe you bit your tongue and grimaced as you said, "I like myself." Could it be because you have been conditioned to feel such an expression is egotistical? Or perchance you find it hard to like yourself. If you did that, though, at least you're off to an excellent start, I hope.

Now become downright audacious. Say, "I like myself, one, I like myself, two, I like myself, three, I like myself, four"—clear up to twenty. Stop reading and do exactly that.

How was it? I trust you're still with me, because this does sound strange. But so did riding a bike, driving a car, and doing a thousand and one other things when you were doing them for the first few times. Call this auto-suggestion if you want to, but if you keep telling yourself, "I like myself," sooner or later, deep down inside, you'll like yourself!

The Mindrobics Prescription

Now here's a four-point Mindrobics prescription. I challenge you to follow it for three weeks, twenty-one days. Now, don't criticize until you utilize.

Number one: Once a day, look at yourself in a mirror, and with all the conviction you can muster, tell yourself out loud, "I like myself, one, I like myself, two," all the way to twenty. Once a day will suffice.

Number two: In bed at night, just before you fall asleep, count off twenty repetitions of "I like myself." Don't move your lips, because it's rather difficult to fall asleep when your lips are moving. Say it silently to yourself over and over at least twenty times. When you reach twenty, keep on going until you fall asleep. For those of you who have other bedtime regimens like prayer or quoting the Bible or other inspirational literature to yourself, this self-affirmation strategy will not interfere.

There is a sound reason for this approach. Your sub-conscious mind works all night long. That's where dreams come from, so if you say, "I like myself, one," etc., all the way, and you keep going and counting off, it's like affirmative counting of sheep. When you fall asleep, that thought of "I like myself" will be in your mind, and your subconscious mind will absorb that all night long.

Number Three: When you wake up in the morning, before you climb out of bed, once again count off twenty repetitions silently to yourself. Why do it silently once again? Because the subconscious mind is also extremely alert in the morning.

Number Four: Throughout the day, when you're driving, when you're mowing your yard, when you're exercising, run the phrase, "I like myself," through your mind. "I like myself." Do twenty repetitions here and there throughout the day.

Given enough time, a minimum of three weeks, these Mindrobics exercises will literally change how you feel about yourself. It's confession time. A few years ago I doubt if you could have found many with lower self-esteem than mine. Like the Prodigal Son of the Bible, I "came to myself" and decided enough was enough. I began using this technique, and it works. I actually like Steve Simms! Pull yourself out of the pits and practice the positives.

Why does Mindrobics make people happy? Why does the "I-like-myself" technique have a positive effect on a person? One reason is because of the mind-over-matter theory of happiness. Of course, that goes, "If you don't mind, it don't matter" In other words, if you think you're happy, then you're really and truly happy. Everybody else may think you're miserable, but you can become a "happychondriac." If you are convinced you're happy, and if you persuade yourself you do like yourself, then isn't that the reality you're after?

The Power of Words

The power of words is another reason that Mindrobics works. Words are the most powerful drug used by mankind. Words can heal or hurt. The sacred books of every world religion deal at length with the strength of words to bless or curse. "Sticks and stones may break my bones, but names [or words] can never hurt me" has been recited in schools and on playgrounds for centuries, but that isn't completely true. When people take bad names or words, and then dwell on them, they can hurt and destroy.

Rudyard Kipling, once known worldwide as Great Britain's poet laureate, wrote, "Not only do words infect, egotize, narcoticize, and paralyze, but they enter into and color the minutest cells of the brain." If you repeat the words, "I like myself. I like myself," they will have an effect on you. You may not see that effect immediately, but the principle will be at work all the while.

Aldous Huxley, renowned English author-philosopher, observed, "Words are magical in the way they affect the minds of those who use them. 'A mere matter of words,' we say, forgetting that words have the power to mold men's thinking, to canalize their feelings, and to direct their feeling and acting."

Instead of repeating "I like myself," all too many denigrate themselves with, "Nobody likes me." They are using negative Mindrobics but not doing it consciously. They constantly groan, as did Mrs. Rubble, "Oh, things never go my way. Nothing ever turns out right for me. I'm such a poor excuse for a human being." They are making themselves unhappier and unhappier by using the Mindrobics principle in reverse.

Happy people avoid running themselves down. Neither do they become obnoxious with braggadocio and egotism. But they do believe and affirm, if only to themselves, "Oh, I'm a good person. I like myself. Matters generally work out right for me."

The Principle of Repetition

Repetition is another valid reason why Mindrobics is effective. The law of repetition emphasizes that: (1) a simple message, hammered at you time and again, will change your attitude, and (2) what you repeat, you begin to believe. Thus, if you repeat a phrase or an idea again and again, it begins to transport itself from your head to your heart, where it no longer merely involves your intellect but begins to influence your inner passions and desires.

At first, when you start to use affirmative, positive statements, they feel weird. They seem to ring with phoniness. I am not asking you to repeat lies, of course. Yes, sometimes you may feel hatred toward yourself, but it is perfectly honest for you to like yourself and to articulate it. Now, men, if you look in the mirror and repeat "I'm God's greatest gift to women," that may not be completely true, even though you may come to believe it! Women, it's wonderful to like yourself—even to love yourself—but try not to worship yourself! Eventually, if you'll persist in honest, positive affirmations, they will become real to you.

$500 to $500,000,000

John H. Johnson is the founder of *Ebony* magazine. It is thought he is worth approximately a half-billion dollars. Yet, he started with nothing but himself. He started his magazine by borrowing $500. To seal the deal, he had to have collateral. He had none, so his mother graciously put up her furniture for the collateral.

Johnson was not a gambler but rather a risk-taker. The risk-taker sticks his neck out for what he believes in. Johnson built a gigantic publishing empire worth $500,000,000 with $500. He was once asked the secret of his success. His reply? "The secret of my success is that I have read Dale Carnegie's book, *How to Win Friends and Influence People,* at least fifty times."

Now you may have read that book once or twice at the most. There is the principle of repetition. It was repeated so often in Johnson's mind that he believed it with all his being and put those principles into practice to the tune of incredible success.

Did you know a bee has to visit about 55,000 clover heads in order to make a pound of honey? Each clover head has about 60 flower tubes. That is a total of 3 1/3 million flower tubes for each pound of honey! That's repetition.

Bundle of Nerves to Powerhouse of Excitement

One of my Nashville friends is Jim Dale, also a motivational-inspirational speaker. He also uses Mindrobics, although he doesn't call it that. He has what he calls his sentence. When Jim began his speaking career, he recalls waiting in a back room with another speaker before they were called to make their entrance onto the stage.

The other speaker was extremely nervous. The fellow shakily remarked, "I'm a bundle of nerves every time I have to make a speech about anything," and walked out to speak. That sentence sank into Jim, and he began thinking about it: "I'm a bundle of nerves every time I have to make a speech about anything."

As I have mentioned more than once, it's dangerous to think . . . but as Jim thought, he became more nervous. Then he asked himself, "What can I do with this sentence? A bundle of nerves. I'm not a bundle of nerves. I'm a human being. I'm a powerhouse of excitement!" So, in his mind Jim changed "bundle of nerves" to "a powerhouse of excitement."

The original phrase also contained "every time I have to make a speech." Jim reasoned with himself, "Wait a minute. I don't have to make a speech. Nobody's making me do this. I'm getting to share from my heart." He changed the sentence to "I am a powerhouse of excitement every time I share from my heart."

The "bundle-of-nerves" sentence also had the phrase "about anything." Jim's brain continued to roll on. He addressed himself, "I don't make speeches about anything. I share from my heart about the things that turn me and my hearers on." Let's repeat that original sentence: "I'm a bundle of nerves every time I have to make a speech about anything." Wow, if you reiterated that enough times, wouldn't you be nervous as a long-tailed cat in a room full of rocking chairs?

What is considered the number-one fear among Americans? Death? Nope. Would you believe public speaking? The fear of death runs second, so public speaking, even before a small group, is dreadful for a huge cross-section of Americans. Why? Because they speak to themselves about being "a bundle of nerves every time I [they] have to make a speech about anything." Follow Jim Dale's method and turn those defeating declarations around. Here is his revised sentence: "I am a powerhouse of excitement every time I share from my heart about the things that turn me on." Why not repeat it a few 100,000 times?

Of course, you will never discover if these techniques will help unless ... you try them. As Jim did, transform the negative expressions and thoughts to positives. Repeat the good stuff at least twenty times a day. You might learn to like yourself, even love yourself.

I have a friend who was the smallest child in the first three grades of grammar school. This was years ago, and he was the only kid in the entire school who was left-handed and wore glasses. To boot, he was cross-eyed. Boys and girls lined up to pick on him before school, during recess, and after school. Finally, at the age of eleven, he decided, "If this keeps up, you're not gonna live. No matter how scared you are, you're gonna take a stand. You're gonna be brave." He repeated that to himself again and again. "I'm gonna be brave. I'm gonna quit hiding behind my glasses and size. I'm gonna be brave." When the next big bully came along, my friend hauled off and hit him in the belly and then bloodied his nose. In the language of evangelical Christians, my friend was, in an emotional sense, "born again." Joe practiced Mindrobics for survival and victory. The school "wimp" went on to box and become an amateur "jock," all because he began thinking Mindrobically.

The Last-Thought Principle

One phase of Mindrobics I have decided to call the last-thought principle. My mind works all night long on the last thought I have before falling asleep. My subconscious ruminates on it, almost as a cow would chew her cud. When I go to bed angry, I wake up in the morning with that anger amplified. I'm usually even more angry. If I fall asleep frustrated, the next AM that condition is expanded.

When you park your car at night, turn off the ignition, and lock the doors, your car sits there idle, doing absolutely nothing until you crank it up again the following day. Not so with your mind. When you park your mind at night by going to sleep, it keeps right on revving up and running. And what is your mind doing when you're asleep?

Of course, there are several factors that influence what it does, but the most pivotal one is the last-thought principle. That means that the last conscious thought before falling asleep will strongly influence the content of your mind's activity throughout the night, and usually that last thought will be amplified in the morning.

If you think positively, perhaps doing those twenty repetitions before going to sleep, it will make a difference in how you get up in the morning. Instead of waking up grouchy, I now arise feeling positive and good, because the last thought in my mind the night before was positive.

You can literally create the emotions you want in the morning. If you don't want to use an entire affirmation or a complete sentence like Jim Dale's sentence or even "I like myself," you can single out one word like love, joy, peace, or happiness and silently repeat that word as you are falling asleep. You'll wake up with happy thoughts the next morning. And even if it's raining, hailing, sleeting, or snowing, you might even burst into the chorus of "Oh, What a Beautiful Morning."

If you're in sales you may want to repeat the word "sales" a number of times before drifting into dreamland. You'll wake up thinking sales and success. I am convinced, through my own experiences and those of others, that you can wake up in whatever frame of mind you desire—unless, of course, you are ill—by using the last-thought principle.

Mental Practice

Another aspect of Mindrobics is mental practice. In *Psychocybernetics*, a classic in the self-help field, Maxwell Maltz refers to a study of three groups of people who were practicing basketball free throws. One group was instructed to practice free throws in their minds only; another, on the court; and another that did not practice at all. The group that practiced in their minds fared as well as the group that practiced by actually shooting free throws on the court. The final percentages of those who practiced by sitting and thinking had the same final effect as actual shooting of the ball.

A psychologist at Marquette University, Anees Seikh, has commented, "Research has shown that mental practice has the same effect as real practice." "There can be no question that mental rehearsal of future events brings results," the author Charles Garfield has remarked.

No doubt you have noticed the concentration of athletes as they are preparing for an event. I can think of nothing more pulse-pounding than the tension on the free-throw shooter in basketball, especially if the outcome of the game is riding on his shots, or the field-goal kicker in football when that three-pointer may mean the difference between winning or losing, or the Olympic athlete under scrutiny right down to a fraction of a point, when 9.75 beats 9.74.

Before the actual free throw, kick, or other event, they may close their eyes, often praying but also in their mind's eye seeing the ball going through the hoop or through the goal-post uprights or viewing that perfect double axal in ice skating. They are visualizing the results they want—I firmly believe two-thirds of one's skill is in programming one's mind to achieve the desired end. Haven't you done the same? In the video player of your mind, you've seen anticipated results, whether in your work, your relationships, your hobbies, your civic responsibilities. Maybe you have even mentally prepared your acceptance speech or rehearsed your sales presentation.

I fear no contradiction at this point: people who succeed use Mindrobics, whether or not they are aware of it. Call it whatever you will—meditation, visualization, imaging, or "psyching oneself up."

For example, Chinese pianist Liu Chi Kung placed second in a 1958 international competition. A year later the Chinese government put him in jail for a seven-year sentence. Although Liu Chi Kung never played a keyboard in jail, he was on tour within months after his release. According to critics, he was playing the piano better than ever. This remarkable man was a world-class pianist. Without touching a piano for seven years, how could he possibly return to his concerts and play more brilliantly than ever? How did he do it without the physical practice?

Kung explained it: "I practiced every day. I rehearsed every piece I had ever played, note by note, in my mind." He visualized a keyboard in his mind—all eighty-eight keys—and he moved his fingers as he visualized the grand piano in his mind. He heard Brahms, Chopin, Tchaikovsky, and more in the concert hall between his ears.

Again I quote Charles Garfield. "Mental rehearsal can provide a tremendous boost to performance. We now know that for a fact." Although mental rehearsal is no substitute for action, it is a necessary preparation for action. Yes, you must finally take action—as I have established throughout—but mental rehearsal is a genuine performance enhancer. Mental rehearsal is a means of reprogramming your mind to achieve more positive results, feelings, and behaviors. It calls on your subconscious mind as an ally as you pursue your goals and desires. Henry Miller said, "Every time you throw home a mental suggestion, whether it's words or pictures, you are giving your subconscious mind a blueprint to go by."

In a sense we have two minds within us—the conscious mind that is always alert and active, except when we are asleep or have impairment; and we have the deep recesses of the mind, the unconscious area or function.

The Superlative Results of Mindrobics

What, then, will Mindrobics do for you and me? Why are affirmation and mental rehearsal essential? Because they put one in touch with the deeper recesses of one's mind. They cause those deep-down desires to merge with one's conscious mind and then translate into successful action. I repeat this on purpose: If you don't program your own mind, if you don't "wash" your own brain, then society and the outward environment will do it. And this often-negative environment will program you how? Negatively. Happy people have used Mindrobics to program themselves for success and victory, not failure and defeat.

There are three aspects of affirmations. Think of Jim Dale's rewritten sentence and one I use: "I like myself." Of course, you not only should think affirmations, but you should write them down. However you want to feel, you can make an affirmation about that.

Write the affirmations in the first person. First person would be the I. Instead of, "Someone else likes me," you write and say, "I." "I am a supersalesman." That's an affirmation I use. I—first person.

So you make them about yourself in first person. Second, you make them in the present tense. Instead of writing or saying, "I am going to like myself," you affirm, "I like myself. I am a super-salesperson"—present tense.

Third, you make your affirmations concise. You do not want to drag them out to infinity.

Another affirmation I have used to help with my self-esteem is, "I am always confident. I am always confident."

You have already practiced Mindrobics but perhaps were not aware of it. Nothing in this chapter is that revolutionary to you, is it? Why not determine to consciously employ the principles of Mindrobics. You'll be happier for it. And those around you will, too.

Right now write five affirmative statements about yourself based on the three suggestions above: first person, present tense, and concise. Then with determination try out Mindrobics for—you already guessed it—three weeks!

Things turn out best for the people who make the best of the way things turn out.
— Art Linkletter

A world without dreams and hopes is no world at all.
— Aretha Franklin

The only way to catch a cold is to chase one.
— Helen Carry

18

CONSCIOUSLY CHOOSE OPTIMISM VS. PESSIMISM

THE AMERICAN INSTITUTE for Preventive Medicine conducted a survey to determine the top ten healthiest New Year's resolutions for 1991. Dr. Don Powell, President of that Detroit-based institute, announced that the number-one New Year's goal for 1991 was to avoid a bad attitude.

Stare reality in the face. Shouldn't that rate high for you and me every year?

Dr. Powell remarked in connection with the announcement: "We used to think that health was from the neck down, but now we see it as more of an integration of mind and body. It's the way we view the events in life." Powell, the author of the book *365 Health Hints,* also reminded his hearers, "You have to look at your attitude, the way you deal with stress, whether you have a social support network, and the way you view life." Dr. Powell, I couldn't agree with you more.

You have stayed with me this far. I fervently hope this book is translating into principles and techniques for your happiness now and from now on out. As we are stretching for the finish line together, there are certain truths I want to re-emphasize.

The Plague of Pessimism

Sure enough, many people are not happy because they are avowed pessimists. They seem to glory in being dismal and down and out. They love martyrdom. And they can't stand to see other people happy. In almost every group, at least one guy is always down, thinking, like Chicken Little, "the sky is going to fall"—and also that the bottom is falling out of everything. Unfortunately, that person is usually sitting on his or hers! Still, even though pessimism is, by its nature and definition, apparently bad, I've personally thought about becoming a pessimist myself. After all, there are . . .

Advantages to Being a Pessimist?

1. *A pessimist doesn't have to worry about pleasing his friends, because he won't have many, if any!*

2. *A talented pessimist can manipulate his family and his coworkers with his pouting.* If you're a pessimist, you can sometimes, by being blue and whining, make folks do what you want them to do.

3. *A pessimist has a built-in excuse for failure.* After all, he knew he couldn't do it—he couldn't make it, he couldn't achieve, he couldn't be successful—even before he started. He reminds you of Don Gibson's old country song, "Born Loser," which goes: "I'm a loser, born loser, I'm a loser, everytime." Isn't that convenient? The pessimist doesn't have to feel bad about failure all the time because he expects it.

4. *A pessimist can develop a reputation as a predictor—even a seer or 'psychic"—of the future.* When things go wrong in someone's life, as of course they sometimes will, the pessimist can pat that person on the back, and say, "See there, I told you it wouldn't work out."

5. *Amazingly, many pessimists are sometimes successful and even notable, in spite of themselves.* For example, Robert Millikan, the 1923 winner of the Nobel Prize in physics, erroneously predicted, "There is no likelihood that man can ever tap the power of the atom." Fortunately or unfortunately, according how you look at it, it was done.

Lord Calvin, who was the president of the British Royal Society in 1895, declared: "Heavier-than-air flying machines are impossible." It's good that the Wright brothers didn't listen to his pessimism.

Many sportswriters in 1921 wrote, "Babe Ruth made a big mistake when he gave up pitching." Of course, Babe didn't listen to that pessimism and became one of the greatest hitters of all time.

This one tops them all. In 1889 the director of the U.S. Patent Office flatly declared, "Everything that can be invented, has been invented." Fortunately for us, that is not at all the case. It is estimated that mankind has accumulated more knowledge and invented more in the last two decades than in all of previous human history put together. Admittedly, notable pessimists have existed.

Become an Incurable Optimist

In spite of those reasons for being a pessimist, though, I've decided against it. After all, with my luck, being a pessimist probably wouldn't work out. Even though Winston Churchill complained of depression, this quote is attributed to him: "I'm an optimist. It just doesn't make much sense being anything else." I agree 1,000 percent.

I hope somewhere in your reading you have made a conscious, willful decision to be an incurable optimist. There is an old story from the early days of baseball, back when folks would drive their T-Models, A-Models, and horses and buggies behind the outfield, sit in their conveyances, and watch the game. One time a car drove up behind the young center fielder, and the driver asked him, "Kid, what's the score?"

He replied, "They got us 56 to 0."

"Good grief," the driver blurted out. "Fifty-six to 0! That's terrible!"

To which the outfielder replied, "Shucks, ain't nothin'. We ain't had our bat yet!" That's optimism!

Characteristics of Pessimists

Unhappy people try to deal with three kinds of trouble at one time—all the trouble they have had, all the trouble they have now, and all the trouble they expect to have in the future—and they try to do it all in one fell swoop. No wonder they're in the pits.

The difficulty with that harum-scarum approach is that troubles are like infants. They grow stronger by nursing, and if you nurse your troubles they're simply going to grow bigger and bigger and cry louder and louder and demand more and more attention. Troubles are like flypaper. They defy the law of gravity and are far easier to pick up than they are to drop.

Still, in spite of that, it would appall you how many people are fond of trouble. Yes, all of us are going to have a certain amount of trouble, but we don't have to cultivate it. Many trouble-lovers run halfway out to meet it. They frantically search for trouble, and if they don't find it, they actually become depressed over it.

Pessimists often feel bad if they even start to feel good. Why? Because they're afraid they're going to feel even worse if they begin to feel better!

Of course, if you know a pessimist rather well, he is the ideal guy to borrow money from, because he doesn't expect you to pay him back anyhow—since he doesn't trust anybody. A pessimist is a person with a nice, even, predictable disposition, miserable all the time.

How can you recognize a true pessimist? A dyed-in-the-wool pessimist is one who receives a clean bill of health from his doctor, but he is so pessimistic that he goes to another doctor, hoping the first doctor's optimistic opinion was wrong. A "genuine" pessimist is deathly afraid that somehow, somewhere, someone's having a good time. And, of course, pessimists are always worried about the economy. A pessimist simply doesn't realize, that if you laid all the economists in the world end to end, they would still point in different directions.

I can hear a pessimist rebutting me with, "Steve, you shouldn't be making fun of our troubles. Troubles are serious concerns, and without troubles, we pessimists would be out of business." I hardly agree with that. A thoroughgoing pessimist can grumble for days if they don't have any troubles.

Nipping Pessimism in the Bud: Positives and Negatives

This is only a matter of review. I have stressed how essential it is that you engineer your attitude. One of the best methods, of course, is to select carefully what you say to yourself, your self-talk. You can actually talk yourself into a frame of mind. No joke. Learn to select words and phrases that convey affirmative, positive approaches. "I hate that" or "I feel bad" are negative, emotive expressions.

148

If you continue those expressions over and over, as we have seen throughout this book, you will program your mind to harbor the emotions of hatred and feeling bad in your mind.

Another self-talk you need to avoid like the plague is negative-predictive talk. That sort of "bluespeak" can lock a person into almost uninterrupted unhappiness.

Examples of negative-predictive talk are such as: "Get down off that ladder. You're going to fall and break your neck." "We're going to have a depression." "We're going to go bankrupt." "We're going to have a wreck." "I just know I'm going to be sick." I could fill up a book with these "we're going tos" or "you're going tos" or "they're going tos." It almost seems that sort of talk contains the portent and promise of calamity. True, it may happen, but you don't have to make it a self-fulfilling prophecy.

Predictive language causes one's mind to shift as if bad has already occurred. As one predicts dire catastrophes, he expects them, braces himself for them—and may secretly lick his chops in anticipation of them. To put it mildly, that is destructive thinking.

Happy, positive people avoid negative-emotive and negative-predictive language. They don't keep on programming themselves for the bad until, sure enough, it happens.

Let me paraphrase a prohibition: Don't react until you're hit. Don't make foreboding predictions. Then, if the negative happens, you have to deal with it, but why predict it?

Another taboo among happy people is: Steer clear of negative absolutes—for instance, "I just never seem to do anything right" (you know better than that!); "I've always been a natural-born loser" (you haven't—who told you that?); and "I'm doomed to failure" (who says so?). Never use negative absolutes like always, never, and nothing.

With negative absolutes pessimists often try to inflict guilt on others, sometimes family members, other relatives, or friends. "You never come and see me." "You ignore me all the time." "If you loved me, you'd let nothing stand in your way." Are those statements true? Never means absolutely never. All the time implies that there is never a time when that is not the case. So if you employ that kind of talk, you are at least a borderline pessimist. You're setting yourself up to feel bad and to read your "bluesprints."

Underline it. Happy, positive people do not make a practice of negative-emotive or negative-predictive language. They put a guard on their self-talk.

Opt for Optimism

Since the late 1930s , Maxwell House Coffee has used the slogan, "Good to the last drop." Folgers has made an institution out of, "The best part of waking up is Folgers in your cup." I'd like to change that to, "The best part of waking up is another day's cup of life, so fill it up to the rim with heartfelt enthusiasm, and do all in your power to make your own life good to the last drop—in so doing, you'll make it better for others, too!"

Personal Happiness—Quality of Thoughts and Attitudes

Relish it. Feast on it. Chew on it. The key to personal happiness is the quality of your thoughts and attitudes. It's not the result of owning and using certain products. Otherwise we could buy happiness, and it's not for sale.

The media have projected an image problem on the entire nation. The brilliantly colored, stereophonic, thirty-second commercial-byte myths that dance around our homes are make-believe. Lying, living-room legends sell us a bill of goods that good times on the TV tube or on the movie screen will materialize when the cash register rings or sings.

Only today as I parallel parked, I noticed a "junker" car behind me. It had seen its better days—too old to be new but not old enough to be antique! On its punctured, twisted grill was a cardboard sign. I think the owner had a sense of humor, because drawn with a Magic Marker was a Mercedes-Benz logo. But the only designer signature you'll ever see on personal happiness ...is your own signature!

Despite all that cities like New York, Hollywood, Rome, and Paris, and streets like Rodeo Drive, Seventh Avenue, Fifth Avenue, and the Champs de Elysees have tried to make us believe ... the only way to be happy is to be happy with yourself.

After all, you never can be happy without you, so make the most of yourself, because that's all there is of you.

One of my favorite Russians, Count Tolstoy, wisely observed, "Everybody thinks of changing the world, but nobody thinks of changing himself." And Charles Wagner expressed what TV's images do not reveal: "Joy is not in things. It is in us." If we are to experience happiness, then we are to experience it within.

Happy people don't have a magic formula that they ordered for $19.95 plus $3.95 postage and handling. Their happiness doesn't magically spring from their designer clothing, their luxury car, their mansion, their $1,000-an-ounce perfume, or their wealth in securities, stocks, bonds, properties, and IRAs ... but from their day-by-day determination to assume control of their thoughts and emotions, deciding to make the world around them brighter because they themselves radiate and reflect light.

True happiness is homemade. Why don't you mix up a batch and start baking today?

There are two ways to make a job an agreeable one. You can change the job so that it agrees with you, or you can change your own attitudes so that you agree with it.

— Joseph A. Kennedy

No one can do his best work when unhappy in heart, or when thinking unhappy thoughts.

— George Matthew Adams

No one can deliver the goods if his heart is heavier than the load.

— Frank Irving Fletcher

19

HAPPINESS IN THE WORKPLACE

I SUSPECT YOU WORK at a job somewhere now, or if you are retired, you did in the past. Maybe you are between jobs or cannot presently locate a job. Perhaps you have your own business or work at home. What's my point, anyhow? That nearly everybody is either working at something now or they have in the past or they hope to in the future.

Enjoy!

You want to work and to be productive, and you want a certain amount of achievement and success, or you wouldn't have read this far. So, why not make up your mind to enjoy your work? Why be unhappy forty or more hours a week? Why try to be happy elsewhere but unhappy in your job?

Sometimes too much stock is put in the polls. For instance, a polling organization might ask a cross-section of only 300 Americans, "How do you feel about the economy?" and then issue front-page statements that "the vast majority of Americans believe we are headed for a depression"—yet only 300 out of 260 million people were polled. But perhaps hundreds of Roper and Gallup polls have asked the question, "Are you happy with your job?" In nearly every case at least 50 percent or more have answered, "No!" They also confidentially reveal that they would love to change their present job for a different one. Why do you think Friday through Sunday is the favorite period for most workers and Monday morning is the most hated? It reminds you of the Carpenters's "Rainy Days and Mondays Always Get Me Down."

Eight Ways to Enjoy Your Work

Here are eight Mindrobics techniques that will help you enjoy your work.

1. *Make up your mind to enjoy it, come hail or high water.* Even if your boss acts like Atilla the Hun or Ivan the Terrible, decide, "I'm gonna feel good, even if nobody else does."

Why not approach your work with this attitude? "Hey, I need to do this work. It's reciprocal. They pay me, and I pay them with my work. I need to support myself (and your dependents if you have them). It's a requirement, so I might as well enjoy it." Isn't that better than, "Oh, man, another lousy day. This is awful." If that's your attitude, no wonder you're unhappy with your work.

A halfway reasonable employer, of course, will like for you to enjoy your work, because when you do, you'll do a better job for her or him. That's the first step.

2. *Maintain good, friendly relationships with your employer and your fellow workers.* In most companies a team spirit is emphasized. Unfortunately, many employees want to grandstand and often build a barrier between themselves and their coworkers. In the long run, that will boomerang on the uncooperative showoff. It helps to have fun, if at all possible, with the employees around you. Encourage them. Look for their good points. If you do—even if aspects of your job are distasteful—you can look forward to interchange with the friends you've made. As you head out to work you'll be thinking, "I can hardly wait to see my friends. Maybe there are some minuses about my workplace, but my fellow workers are not one of them."

3. *Remember that your work provides much, if not all, of your necessities and luxuries.* Unless you inherited a bundle or somehow you're independently wealthy, you owe your means of livelihood to your work. When you think about that, maybe the job doesn't look

quite as bad. Your work is at least helping you make it. Always bear in mind that your work helps pay the bills and sometimes makes your "fun things" possible, even if that means going to a fast-food restaurant once a week or bowling or catching a movie or renting a videotape for the VCR you bought with your salary.

4. *Keep in mind the service you provide people through your work. You're providing some sort of service to somebody.* You are serving either by offering goods (and the maintenance of those goods) or services. Thinking of your work as a service makes a vast difference between a feeling of drudgery or one of dedication. Whether you are a surgeon or a shoe salesman, you are helping people, and that should make life exhilarating.

5. *Challenge yourself at work.* This will put pizzazz into your job and multiply your happiness. Yes, a certain amount of progress may be accidental, but it's far more satisfying to plan for it. Envision your dreams and goals and then celebrate when, one by one, they become realities.

Once I had a job doing nothing but inventory in retail stores. You may love that sort of work, but to me it was a drag. All I did hour after hour was run a calculator to count merchandise on shelves. It was like counting beans.

And yet, I set a goal to raise my average of counting higher and higher. I even became rather excited as I was able to inventory more and more in less and less time. It became a game of challenge as I tried to beat my previous total—and did. So if you'll stretch yourself and always try to do a little bit better, that technique can make even a blah job, exciting.

6. *Concentrate on the good things about your job.* Believe it or not, there must be something you like about your job. You may protest, "Well, Steve, I hate everything about my job." I don't believe that.

Is your job in a building? If it is, you can reply, "Yeah, it's in a building." I would then ask, "Would you rather work outside in all kinds of weather? Is the building heated and air-conditioned?" If "yes" is your answer, "Would you rather work without air-conditioning and heating?" "Do they pay you for your job?" If you say, "yes," "Would you rather work without pay?"

Underline this. You can find something you like about your job, even if all you like about it is the fact you get paid. Maybe you like some of your benefits or even appreciate your vacation.

Why not make a list of ten things you like about your job?

7. *Do more than you're paid to do.* That doesn't sound enjoyable, does it? Yet, it can be. Far too many workers do barely enough to squeak by. They start work on the dot or late, and they leave on the exact minute or early.

But people who just do barely enough to get by seldom get ahead. If you put something extra into your work, it will show. Somewhere along the line, discerning management will notice and reward you. Chances are if you do more than you are paid for, you will end up being paid more for what you do.

8. *Adopt the attitude of "This is my company."* Since you earn all or part of your living at your workplace, why not cultivate a sense of pride and achievement in your business or company? Sure, you may not actually own the company where you work, but in a real sense, it is your company. You are a part of it; you are identified with it. For instance, I don't own a single brick of the school where I went to high school, but years later, I still have the feeling that is is my high school. Develop that feeling for your company, government agency, or organization where you work. You're a part of it, and when you begin to feel it's your company, you'll have a sense of genuine belonging and even ownership. Going to work will assume a vibrant meaning.

Motivation Is a Must

Motivation may sound fancy. All in the world it means, bottom line, is having the inward desire or urge that impels one to act, to do, to move, to achieve, to succeed at a goal. There's the mystery of motivation. It's an internal need that's satisfied by an external expression.

Sure enough those eight techniques toward liking our jobs more will help us become more motivated, but there are other catalysts that can propel us. When you experience happiness and success, and you want more, that's motivation. The truly motivated person wants to act to achieve what he wants or either avoid what he doesn't want.

A Motivation Trio

There are three prime ways to motivation. Number one is the "KITA" Method of Motivation. It stands for "Kick In The Anatomy." KITA is based on the fear of punishment if one doesn't respond as anticipated or expected. It motivates one to recoil from that which is painful or distasteful. It reminds you of the old prison days where the convicts busted rocks, not because they got their jollies from that, but if they didn't they would have been "busted" senseless.

One example of the KITA method is when the boss threatens to fire you unless you stop showing up for work late. He might express it, "Steve, if you don't start being here on time all the time, you're gonna be history." In other words, he's going to can me, fire me, "surplus me," or "make my position redundant." That's KITA. If I really value my job, I'll bust a gut to be there on time.

The second motivation technique is **The Four Ps Principle**. This principle employs **praise, prestige, promotion**, and/or **paycheck** to motivate people. The Four Ps pull employees toward achievements, aims, and goals by promising various rewards for taking action.

An example of the Four Ps would be this, "Steve, you're too good of an employee to be late for work all the time. Now, when you start to be punctual, and you show up on time for an entire month, I'm going to give you a promotion and a raise. And not only that, I'll announce it in the company newsletter." There are the Four Ps as motivators. The boss promised a promotion and a raise in pay, along with subsequent praise and publicity. I hope your boss is like that. That sort of treatment would compel, impel, and propel most employees to do better, not out of fear, but out of appreciation and anticipation of reward.

The KITA and the Four Ps principles of motivation both work, but they're not as effective as the third method, and that's the entire point of this book. The third method is Self-Motivation. It has no particular name. It involves discovering a personal reason, deep down in yourself, for taking effective action. Self-motivation will call for all the Mindrobics techniques we have examined in this book.

Unfortunately, most of our fellow earthlings pass through life being pushed or pulled by outward circumstances. They do most of what they do in response to what happens to them. They're like a billiard ball. They're bouncing off the rails of life or falling into the

157

pockets all in response to the positive or negative cues of their outward environment.

An effectively motivated person, though, is motivated how? By himself, not like a wheelbarrow being pushed, not like one of Pavlov's conditioned-reflex dogs, not like a naughty child afraid of being punished.

Instead, a dynamically motivated person is like an automobile. He or she is driven by his own power source from within. This person has learned to apply the principles of Mindrobics to the extent he can move and act productively on his own.

We can do anything we want to do if we stick with it long enough.

— Helen Keller

You may be whatever you resolve to be.

— Stonewall Jackson

Confidence is the magic key that unlocks the door of supply.

— Orison Swett Marden

20

GO FOR IT!

T HERE WAS A TIME when I considered myself a natural-born loser. Every day was a constant pain to my entire being. Now I consider myself a natural-born winner. How and why? My perspective. I sat down and decided: "Steve Simms, you will no longer be your worst enemy. You will be your best friend." I consciously chose to be a winner instead of a loser, an optimist instead of a pessimist, a happy guy instead of a gloomy Gus. If I could do it, you can.

It seems that most people accept whatever life serves them; like GIs in a chow line, they accept, zombie-like, what falls onto their plates. Oh, they may complain or grumble a bit, but in the end they go right ahead and consume a toxic diet of negative attitudes, circumstances, and emotions sloppily splashed onto the "mess kits" of their lives.

Motivated and positive people, however, obtain what they want in life. How do they do it?

Four Basic Techniques for Getting What You Want in Life

1. *Wish for it.* Knowing what you want is always the first step to getting it. Yet, many people have no idea what they want in life. Someone has said, "Unhappiness is not knowing what you want and killing yourself to get it."

Ask many people, "What do you want out of life?" and they'll answer, "Well, I really don't know. Money. A house. An expensive car. Maybe kids. I don't know." And surprisingly many don't seem to give a hoot. But that surely doesn't describe you, does it? Why not dare to dream again?

Before you waste precious time and energy, let your imagination run free. If you could be anything and have anything and do anything you wanted, what would it be? Happy people learn to dream. Children inherently know how to dream, even how to reach for a star. We as adults have forgotten how to dream. You already guessed it: happy people remember how to dream and to wish for what they want.

2. *Fish for it.* When your wish sets in, let action begin. Dig your bait, and bait your hook. Drop your line, and continue casting to realize your dream, to behold it with your naked eyes, to make it real. Positive people go far beyond wishing. They move from wishing to fishing.

3. *Insist on it.* Unfortunately, half-hearted attempts at fishing for your wish seldom prevail. Discouragement knocks on everybody's door. It's easy to give up on a delayed dream—to walk away—to settle for second best. It's easy to assume that your desire is "not meant to be." But positive people refuse to give up. They insist for their wish.

4. *Persist for it.* Wishes seldom, if ever, come true in a flash. Even though you insist, it still may take time, even a long time. If you're broke and somebody tells you you'll be worth a million or more in three weeks, that's a little fast. It may take a lot longer. Happy people realize that, by and large, overnight success is a myth. There are always obstacles, difficulties, and struggles ... and people who get what they want are those persistent pluggers who continue to hold onto their dreams after most everybody else has let theirs evaporate in a puff of smoke. Mary Crowley, the founder of Home Interiors, aptly said, "You may give out, but never give up."

So would you like to get what you want out of life? It's not easy, but it's simple. Wish for it. Fish for it. Insist on it. And persist for it.

The Diet Cola Formula

Another strategy for pointing your life in the direction you want it to go is the Diet Cola Success Formula. I call it that because I remember it as *Tab*. The T stands for think, A for act, and B for be. This formula goes: Think like you want to be. Act like you want to be. Be like you want to be. Is there anything complicated about TAB?

So, how can you begin to employ these techniques? One slogan I have often heard is: If you want to accomplish something in life, just do it. Yet, accomplishment is rarely that simple. Sometimes the just-do-it formula for success just won't do it, and far more is required than a mere positive phrase.

For example, how can I "just do it" when it comes to removing your appendix or to flying a jet plane or to playing for an NBA basketball team when I'm uncoordinated and six feet tall?

Now I could probably learn to perform an appendectomy or even fly a plane, but I honestly doubt if I could make it in the NBA, even if I had thirty-six hours a day to practice. For a fact, the just-do-it formula won't always work.

The How Trio

So what's required for the successful accomplishment of a job, goal, or task? *The How Trio* is necessary. Know-how, feel-how, and do-now.

Know-how involves both knowledge and ability. A person must either know how to accomplish his goal or else have the ability of learning how to do it. For example, I could learn the information I required to fly an airplane, but I probably don't have the basic ability to learn how to be a basketball star. The accumulation of knowledge is a vital ingredient in accomplishment.

Feel-how involves practice. I might know how to fly a plane, but if I've never actually done it, you probably don't want to be on that plane when I taxi down the runway and take off. Merely the fact that I have the knowledge is not enough. In such a case you would want me to have the experience. You may remember "The Beverly Hillbillies." Remember how Jethro often drawled, "Shucks, I wanna be a brain surgeon." Did you ever cringe at the thought of Jethro operating on your gray matter? Well, you'd feel like that if I were your jet pilot. You'd much rather that I have the experience and the necessary flight hours logged.

Remember the rule of twenty-one days I have touched on earlier? Psychologists feel that many days are essential for a new behavior to feel right for a person. New behaviors always seem awkward at first. We have to creep and crawl before we can toddle and walk. "If it's worth doing, it's worth doing lousy until we can learn to do it well."

Happy, positive, successful people have repeatedly put their knowledge and abilities to work until what they do becomes second nature for them, "like breathing out and breathing in," to quote from "My Fair Lady." They do it and they practice it until they "get the hang" of it. That's what I mean by feel-how.

Do-now involves motivation, which we have considered earlier. Do-now is the desire and the willingness to put your know-how and your feel-how to work on a consistent basis. Do-now involves a personal why, an inner reason to take action, and a cause that impels you to get things done.

When you have the know-how to follow through on these techniques, that's good. But then you need the feel-how, and that involves doing them for the three weeks until they start to feel natural. But in order to do that, you need the do-now, the desire to declare, "Yes, I want to be happy. If anybody in this world can be positive and be happy, I can. But I've got to work at it, and so I'm going to take that action."

Can't Have One Without the Other

Do-now without know-how and feel-how causes frustration. If you try to take action, and you don't know how—you haven't had the experience—you can really become baffled and bewildered. Know-how and feel-how without the do-now causes routine and boredom. If you know how to do this or that, but all you do is nothing, you experience boredom. But when you put all parts of the trip together, you have a sure-fire recipe for accomplishment.

Self-inventory

A personal inventory is helpful. Periodically ask yourself:
1. What do I want to accomplish?

162

2. Do I have a positive goal or goals I am excited about pursuing?

3. Do I have enough knowledge and ability to reach them?

4. Do I have the know-how?

5. Have I acquired proficiency in the skills?

6. Have I read this book well enough that I am conversant with the techniques?

7. Am I taking regular, effective, persistent action toward my goal(s), regardless of the obstacles in my way?

8. Am I overcoming the awkwardness that I first had when I tried these techniques, and am I persisting at it?"

If you can answer yes to all those questions, you're headed toward amazing personal happiness and success. If you answered no to part of them, you still may be a hair's breadth from your dreams, goals, and wishes. Perhaps all you lack is for you to amplify these three basic ingredients: know-how, feel-how, and do-now. And you acquire those through study, practice, and inspiration.

Hands on My Time

Oh, you thought it was "Time on My Hands." Not in this case. If I am to have an attitude of happiness and success, I must put my hands on my time. Ben Franklin expressed it well: "Do not squander time, for that's the stuff life's made of." What do you do with time? How do you regard it?

Eight Suggestions on Wise Time Management

1. *Tend to business and not to busyness.* A person can actually be "busy" at his work without accomplishing much of anything except moving papers from one box to another. You see, activity does not necessarily equal accomplishment. In your official work or your work at home, you need to ask yourself, "Do I really need to do this?" before you do it. Try to make sure that what you are doing will move you toward your goal. Place results on value and not many results merely on time and effort alone. Results and value do count.

2. *Accept responsibility for the use of your time.* Rather than blaming others for your pressures, become the commander of your schedule. Do not let the schedule dictate to you. If a schedule or deadline assigned to you seems unreasonable, talk it over with your supervisor and/or other team members. Don't be afraid to say no when it is necessary for efficiency and productivity. Too, nobody

knows better than you what wastes your time and saps your energy. Happy people endeavor not to waste time.

3. *Delegate where possible.* Don't carry other people's workloads. Share tasks with your family members, your employees, your coworkers. Maybe you just feel overworked and complain, "Steve, I just can't be happy. I have too much to do."

Why is that? Could it be you are reluctant to delegate for one of the following reasons? (1) Inability to trust others—what I have chosen to call a form of "professional paranoia." (2) Indispensability—that is, yours. In other words, only you can perform the B or C tasks. How often I have seen busy executives at the copy machine all afternoon. (3) Inertia—that is, deep down inside you want to share responsibility but either you don't know how or you're afraid to.

Yes, do your fair share. Go that second mile, but also learn to let other people help, even if they are not "perfect." Let others do their fair share.

Women sometimes fall into this drudgery routine in their homes, doing everything rather than letting their husbands or children pitch in. Simply because someone else abdicates his or her responsibility, refuse to shoulder it for them. Push it back on them. We are living in a new day. Since more than two-thirds of women are working outside, as well as inside, their homes, they have every right to expect members of the family to pitch in. As a married man with a more flexible schedule than my wife's I often serve as "Mr. Mom."

4. *Put your creativity to work.* Search for more efficient ways and means of getting things done. Use idle time. Learn to do two compatible things at once. What helps me considerably is listening to motivational tapes while I'm driving to and from my speaking engagements. You can also read while you're waiting for a doctor or for a client. I've even known of students who studied and business persons who did reports or committed inspirational mottos and slogans to memory while waiting in long lines.

5. *Inject pleasure into all your activities, whether at work or play.* It's so apparent they didn't have to study it, but studies have shown that people who enjoy what they do are far more efficient and productive than people who don't. As I suggested one time earlier, make a game out of what you're doing and devise even more ideas about how to get a kick out of it. And if you can have fun while you're

working, just think, you can combine this with number 4 above. So, you'll be using your creativity and doing two things at once.

6. *Begin to view time as your friend and not your enemy.* Time's a blessing, not a blight. It's not a stress producer. What you do with time makes the difference. After all, when your time's used up, then you're used up. When your time's gone, you're out of this life. So stay calm about time.

Cherish time because, when you come down to it, it's all you've got. Today more and more workers, if given a choice of "perks," are electing for time. Yes, "time is money, and money is time." But down the pike time is more important.

7. *Keep a strong self-image independent of your work.* You're not Ms. or Mr. Just What You Do. As we have seen, your performance is not a determination of your value as a human being, so avoid perfectionism. Don't always redo a job, striving for perfection. Instead, aim for excellence. There is a difference. Excellence is striving toward superior quality. Simply do your best and then be content with that.

8. *Plan for your priorities.* Then devote the best portion of your time to the matters that are most important to you. Planning is essential if you want to avoid spending time on trivialities that don't matter to you. Planning your time saves time.

The now that existed when I began to voice this word, "hello," has gone forever. Time is moving on. That moment when I said "hello" is gone forever, and it left in a hurry, didn't it? Stop and think about it—but not too long. All our moments flash by speedily.

But counting time is not as important as making time count. The important factor in life is not how old you are, but how you are old; not how much time has passed in your life, but how have you passed your time.

So what's the best use of time? The main purpose of life is to live it, so while you're making a living, don't forget to make a life!

Today I have gotten out of all trouble, or rather I have cast out all trouble, for it was not outside, but within and in my opinion.

— Marcus Aurelius

He who is plenteously provided for from within needs little from without.

— Goethe

Faith is to believe what we do not see, and the reward of this faith is to see what we believe.

— St. Augustine

21

IT'S YOUR PARTY ... AND YOU'LL LAUGH IF YOU WANT TO!

ENJOY YOUR LIFE by savoring the present moment. Except in the most unusual cases, small children have a knack for making life fun. We adults often forget.

Fantastic Formulas

Sadly, most people think of happiness as being in the future. "I'll be happy when ..." "Out there somewhere I'll ..." Because people defer happiness, they miss the abundant, simple pleasure of the here and now.

Discover what you really want out of life, but avoid the path of least resistance. I have heard that failure is the path of least persistence. Someone said: "The greatest pleasure in life is doing what people say you cannot do." Go for it. Do it.

Sincerely love and treat people right. Love even those who are difficult to love. Determine you are going to love those who are cantankerous, unloving, and mean. Maybe they're the way they are because nobody ever expressed love toward them. Give people all the love and kindness that you have, and love and kindness will become blessed boomerangs.

Discard your pet regrets. Live in the present moment, not in the past. Positive people are using time in the present, not looking back at what could have been, what should have been, and not using negatives like "I should," "I wish I had," "I could have," "if only," and their sad "bluespeak" relatives.

Learn to like yourself. Most of mankind's worst problems are caused by those who don't like themselves. People who genuinely feel good about themselves are the most positive and productive people in the world. They don't waste valuable time feeling sorry for themselves, so learn to get along well with yourself, and when you can get along well with you, you'll find you can get along with other people as well.

Reset Your Cruise Control

It is my conviction that all of us as human beings have cruise controls that determine how far and how fast we will go in our lives. Regardless of your outward circumstances, your life will conform to the setting on your personal cruise control.

When you come to a steep hill in life, and you have to climb over major obstacles, your performance will remain generally consistent with your performance on level ground. Personal cruise control will compensate for the obstacles and release enough of your unused ability to maintain roughly the same degree of achievement in your life.

It works like the cruise control on the car. When the car is going uphill, the accelerator puts in more gas. The same speed is maintained. When your circumstances improve and things are going well for you, instead of going faster and increasing your accomplishment, your cruise control cuts back, and you coast along at the same speed as before. It's like when a car starts going downhill, the cruise control doesn't let it go faster. The cruise control maintains the speed. We all have a cruise control inside our mind that is setting our levels of happiness and success.

Let me give you an example. A saleslady made $20,000 her first year in her company's best territory. But that was far below the normal production for that territory, so the company moved her to their worst territory. And the next year she made $20,000, which was the most money ever made in their worst territory. So to reward her, the company transferred her back to the best territory, and in spite of her improved circumstances, the next year she still made $20,000.

The company management, after this, asked her to go to a career counselor. The counselor discovered that the most money her father had ever made was $20,000. The saleslady realized that she would feel guilty if she ever made more than her father. Her personal cruise control was set on $20,000. When she was in the good territory and she achieved that, her "cruise control" caused her to hold back. When she was in the bad territory, her system worked hard to make up for the bad circumstances.

So the counselor helped her to deal with her will and her inward attitude and to change her feelings about her father and about her self-worth. She realized that it was not disrespectful to make more than her father, and she stopped seeing herself as a $20,000-a-year salesperson. She began to see herself as a top producer.

When she reset her inner cruise control, her self-image, her performance level changed as well, and she became a sales leader for the company.

That's what we're after in the Mindrobics concepts of this book. We've been after techniques that can help you readjust your personal cruise control.

People don't only set their cruise controls on how much money they make, but many set their cruise controls on happiness. "I can only be so happy," or, "It's not right," you've heard people remark. And they've added, "This is too good to last." I read a statement some time ago that's helped me tremendously, "Nothing is too good to last." If you're in good times right now, good things are happening to you; it's not too good to last. You deserve it. You see, you can readjust your cruise control so you can dramatically improve your level of functioning. Only these ingredients are necessary — disciplined mental effort, persistence, and time.

Human cruise controls seldom change without long-term mental work, but if you sincerely want to improve your self-image, and if you'll make a long-term effort to reprogram your thinking according to these techniques, you can reset your mental cruise control on happiness and joy, on confidence, on dramatic achievement, on success, on all these other positives.

Other Sources of Help

I'm the first to admit that the techniques we have shared in this book are not foolproof and that there are types of unhappiness, misery, and depression that require clinical help. There's nothing wrong with seeking help. If you use these techniques and you're still not happy, then there's nothing wrong with going for help.

Many optimistic, positive persons have had professional help at times. There's no problem with that.

Back to the Source

It is remarkable that all self-help books go back to one source, although I may not have patently acknowledged this throughout these pages. Before there was Norman Vincent Peale's *The Power of Positive Thinking*, there was, "Finally brethren, whatsoever things are true, honest, just, pure, lovely, if there be any virtue and if there be any praise, think on these things."

Before Dale Carnegie wrote the book, *How to Win Friends and Influence People,* someone had penned these simple words: "Love one another."

Before Claude Bristol authored *The Magic of Believing*, someone had written, "As you believe, so shall it be done unto you."

Before Napoleon Hill came out with *Think and Grow Rich,* these words were set down, "This book of the law shall not depart out of your mouth, but you shall meditate therein both day and night for then you shall make your way prosperous, and then you shall have good success."

Before David Schwartz wrote *The Magic of Thinking Big,* there was, "Where there is no vision, the people perish."

And before Maxwell Maltz released *Psychocybernetics*, someone had written, "Ask and it shall be given you. Seek and you shall find. Knock and the door shall be opened unto you."

Before Zig Ziglar penned *See You at the Top*, there was, "Humble yourself under the mighty hand of God that in due time he may exalt you."

Before David Burns wrote the book, *Feeling Good,* there was "joy unspeakable and full of glory."

Before Frank Bettger's *How I Raised Myself from Failure to Success in Selling*, there was: "By love, serve one another."

And before Irene C. Kassorla wrote the book, *Go for It,* there was a rule: "Let him who does not work, not eat."

All of those pre-existing statements are from the Bible!

Napoleon Hill said, "People will go to a whole lot of trouble to learn a subject, a skill, a profession, a trade, a hobby, but they just don't want to be bothered with learning how to operate themselves."

Now, I trust you've read this entire book, so you're a person who wants to do better, to improve yourself, and to be happy. I highly encourage you to read as many self-help books as you can. The books I have mentioned are among my favorites.

They are powerful and can assist you in addition to the material in this book. In fact, plenty of material in this book was inspired by those volumes. But even more, the material in these books intentionally—and sometimes unintentionally—go back to one book that's the best self-help book I've ever encountered—the Bible. It's not really a religious book. It's a practical, how-to manual on how to operate yourself. You might call the Bible the "Manufacturer's Handbook" for successful and happy human living.

As you've also noticed, I've quoted from Buddha and Confucius, and the story about the farmer's son who broke his leg while riding a horse is from Zen Buddhism. And I have quoted from philosophers like Socrates, Plato, and Epictetus and literary giants like Leo Tolstoy, Emily Dickinson, and Helen Keller.

One of the greatest Mindrobics tools I've found in being happy is to saturate oneself with this material. Years ago a men's hair dressing advertised, "A little dab'll do ya." In being happy, though, I have discovered that a little dab just won't do me. Fill your life with, first of all, positive people—then positive books, tapes, messages, seminars, and media programs.

You can be happy for the rest of your days. I encourage you to be insistent and persistent in being happy. You can engineer a joyous attitude.

Here's wishing you happiness all the days of your life.

Never give up, keep on trying.
Be strong, be brave, be true.
If they can make penicillin out of moldy bread,
You can make something great out of you!
— Author Unknown

STEVE SIMMS

America's Encouragement Engineer

Topics:
- *Lighten Up And Succeed*
- *Don't Lose Your Marbles*
- *The Spirit of Serving Customers*
- *Leadership/Work Styles*

Steve Simms has presented speeches and seminars for associations and companies accross the nation, including:

National Fraternal Congress of America
National Association of Police Athletic Leagues
American Society of Consultant Pharmacists
National Electrical Generating System Association
Colorado, Idaho, Tennessee, West Virginia,
and Texas Municipal Leagues
South Central Bell
Montana, Texas, New Mexico, Tennessee,
and Illinois Health Care Associations
United Cities Gas
Quorum Health Group, Inc.
Chambers of Commerce
Schools and School Boards
International City/County Managers Association

Targeted content, a dynamic speaking style, uplifting humor, and a warm friendly manner make Steve Simms' speeches and seminars a treat for audiences in organizations nationwide.
To discuss scheduling Steve Simms for your upcoming event
call
Attitude -Lifter Enterprises
(615) 791-8777

173

SPREAD THE HAPPINESS!

Order More Copies of
Mindrobics:
How To Be Happy For The Rest Of Your Life

Mindrobics (book)
Please send _____ copies of *Mindrobics* book
@ $12.95 each . . . . $_____
    10 or more — $10.95 each
    50 or more — $8.95 each

Mindrobics (tape series, 6 cassettes, 5 1/2 hours)
Please send _____ copies of *Mindrobics* tape series
@ $59.95 each . . . . $_____

Mindrobics (video, approximately one hour)
Please send _____ copies of *Mindrobics* video
@ $59.95 each . . . . $_____

Don't Lose Your Marbles (single audio cassette)
Please send _____ copies of *Don't Lose Your Marbles* cassette
@ $10.95 each . . . . $_____

SUBTOTAL . . . . $_____
TN residents only — add 8.25% sales tax: . . . . $_____
Shipping — add 5% of order ($3.00 minimum) . . . . . . $_____

TOTAL . . . . $_____

MAIL CHECK TO:
ATTITUDE-LIFTER ENTERPRISES
528 DALE COURT
FRANKLIN, TN 37067
615-791-8777

SPREAD THE HAPPINESS!

Order More Copies of
Mindrobics:
How To Be Happy For The Rest Of Your Life

Mindrobics (book)
Please send _____ copies of *Mindrobics* book
@ $12.95 each . . . . $_____
    10 or more — $10.95 each
    50 or more — $8.95 each

Mindrobics (tape series, 6 cassettes, 5 1/2 hours)
Please send _____ copies of *Mindrobics* tape series
@ $59.95 each . . . . $_____

Mindrobics (video, approximately one hour)
Please send _____ copies of *Mindrobics* video
@ $59.95 each . . . . $_____

Don't Lose Your Marbles (single audio cassette)
Please send _____ copies of *Don't Lose Your Marbles* cassette
@ $10.95 each . . . . $_____

SUBTOTAL . . . . $_____
TN residents only — add 8.25% sales tax: . . . . $_____
Shipping — add 5% of order ($3.00 minimum) . . . . . . $_____

TOTAL . . . . $_____

MAIL CHECK TO:
ATTITUDE-LIFTER ENTERPRISES
528 DALE COURT
FRANKLIN, TN 37067
615-791-8777

177

SPREAD THE HAPPINESS!

Order More Copies of
Mindrobics:
How To Be Happy For The Rest Of Your Life

Mindrobics (book)
Please send _____ copies of *Mindrobics* book
@ $12.95 each . . . . $_____
    10 or more — $10.95 each
    50 or more — $8.95 each

Mindrobics (tape series, 6 cassettes, 5 1/2 hours)
Please send _____ copies of *Mindrobics* tape series
@ $59.95 each . . . . $_____

Mindrobics (video, approximately one hour)
Please send _____ copies of *Mindrobics* video
@ $59.95 each . . . . $_____

Don't Lose Your Marbles (single audio cassette)
Please send _____ copies of *Don't Lose Your Marbles* cassette
@ $10.95 each . . . . $_____

SUBTOTAL . . . . $_____
TN residents only — add 8.25% sales tax: . . . . $_____
Shipping — add 5% of order ($3.00 minimum) . . . . . . $_____

TOTAL . . . . $_____

MAIL CHECK TO:
ATTITUDE-LIFTER ENTERPRISES
528 DALE COURT
FRANKLIN, TN 37067
615-791-8777